THE PARENT AS TEACHER

This book is addressed to:

PARENTS who would like to help their children make the best use of their schooling but don't know how, and are afraid of coming into conflict with what is taught them in school,

TEACHERS who know they haven't the time to give individual help to a child but hesitate to suggest how the parent may help for fear of the anxieties and tensions which the parent's attempts may induce,

VOLUNTEERS who give their services in schools or in community projects and need a clear, structured programme to follow.

COLLEGE STUDENTS who would like to involve themselves usefully in remedial projects in schools or the community and who, like volunteers, will appreciate an explicit and detailed programme of remedial activities.

SCHOOL PSYCHOLOGISTS who require a handy guide to the counselling of parents of children with learning disabilities or behaviour problems, or a simple manual to which they can refer parents.

the Parent as Teacher

A guide for parents of children with learning difficulties

D.H.Stott

new press
Toronto
1972

ISBN 0-88770-676-2 cloth
ISBN 0-88770-677-0 paper

First printing

123456   77   76   75   74   73   72

new press
Order Department
553 Richmond Street West
Toronto 133, Ontario

Design/Pamela Patrick
Manufactured in Canada
Typeset by House of Letters, Toronto
Printed by Alger Press, Oshawa, Ont.

Table of contents

1

The nature of the problem

This is a frustrating world for the parent of the learning-disabled child. No one can honestly claim that as a whole our school systems are coping with the problem adequately. In rural areas where distances are great and taxes are insufficient to support a special-education service little pretence is made to provide help. In a prosperous and advanced civilization such as ours this is a scandalous situation. The unhappiness and the economic waste caused by learning difficulties and their attendant emotional tensions pose a much more direct and poignant problem than that of chemical pollution, yet so far it has been mostly swept under the rug. We have not known what to do about it, and to save face we have regarded it as inevitable.

The purpose of this book is to show that something can be done. When parents realize this I am sure that it will become an issue of equal urgency with that of pollution, because every year's delay means more children passing the age when the most could have been done to help them. Among the hundreds of letters I received following a newspaper article[1] on our work at Guelph, those I was most uneasy and unhappy about were from parents of teenage boys and girls and even of adult sons and daughters who had battled in vain for years in search of a solution. Some mothers wrote to me about sons whose learning disability had ended up in serious crime. Others feared that their children, seeing them so "turned off" by education, would turn to delinquency. Whatever the cause, we have to face the fact that the greatest incidence of juvenile crime is found among young people who have failed in school. Many parents who wrote told me how they had taken their children the rounds of doctors and psychological clinics. Then they had been tested, and in some cases a diagnosis was made—typically that the child was of "low average intelligence" or suffered from "perceptual handicaps" —but no treatment or significant remedial help followed.

What the parent of the learning-disabled child should and should not do The first thing to realize—and I say this at the risk of offending many of my professional colleagues—is that no one can tell you, on the basis of a series of mental tests, what is wrong with your child. Later I shall argue this point at length. Suffice it to say now that all an intelligence test tells us is the extent to which the child is bringing his intelligence to bear on

1. Sheena Paterson, "The Door that Optimism Opened," *Weekend Magazine*, Nov. 6, 1972.

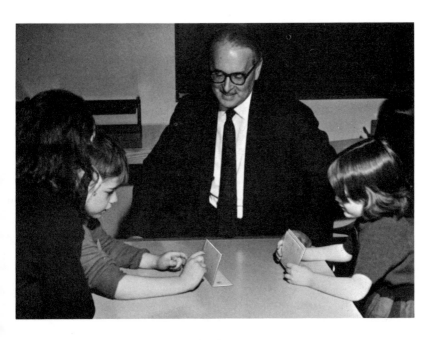

The author tries out a new phonics game with some Kindergarten-age children of volunteers.

the academic type of learning. It does not tell us what intelligence might be revealed if he brought into use what he has, and used it in the right way. His IQ may well reflect his current learning disability, since he probably uses the same faulty tactics in doing the test as caused him to fail in school. After years of misuse his brain will be just as ill-equipped to solve the problems posed in the test as it is to cope with school tasks. At best, therefore, the IQ tells us what we know already, that he is learning-disabled. At worst, it misleads us about what he could achieve if his brain were trained to function properly. A low IQ gives the impression that nothing can be done about his failure because he has not the mental capacity, and so generates discouragement and pessimism. But the IQ is a mere number, which cannot convey the true nature of the disability and in no way gives us guidance on how to deal with it.

This does not mean, of course, that psychological help is useless. What is useless—and possibly harmful— is to take your child around to a series of clinics which hand out diagnoses not followed up by a programme of remedial treatment. The alternative in most cases is to seek help from the psychological service of a school board or a children's hospital that has the facilities to make an ongoing study of your child as he responds to the remedial programme.

I am putting things so strongly because in over twenty years during which I have worked with learning-disabled children I have become convinced that the child's ability to learn can only be discovered progressively in the course of a programme which shows him how to learn. Until a child is using his mind, and using it aright, no one on earth can discover how much ability he has. You as a parent may know more about the "intelligence" of your child than any psychologist can tell you from a test. Many of the parents who have written to me are convinced that their children are not just "dull", despite the low IQ's that they obtain in tests. Psychologists and teachers have tended to brush aside such judgments as parental bias. But I am now sure that the parent has been right in many instances and that we have been wrong.

To write in this vein may appear dangerous to many people. I shall be accused of arousing false hopes. My answer is to ask whether they would ban public knowledge, say, of a treatment of cancer which had been found to cure some sufferers but not others. If many learning-disabled children, and even some at present regarded as mentally retarded, can be rescued from a life of frustration and dependence, surely the truth is worth some risk of disappointment.

Of course we have to be suspicious of cure-alls, especially if they are linked with high clinical fees. What the psychologist should say to the parents who demand tests is, "We cannot tell from the present state of your child what his learning ability may be, or whether we can cure him. All we can do is to bring him into a learning programme and observe how he sets about learning tasks, and is able progressively to correct his faults. Only then will he reveal his abilities". In other words, he can promise nothing but that the child will be given a chance. It may be that after a few months the psychologist has to tell the parent that the child is at the present time too fundamentally disorganized in his behaviour and mental functioning to cope with any academic programme. But at least this will be a realistic assessment based upon a fair trial of the child's abilities.

In one way, however, I have to confess that up to this point I have been unrealistic. There are not enough psychologists, special-education consultants or teachers trained in special education to go round. This is the result of long-standing assumptions that slow-learning children must always remain slow learners because of their low intelligence. Lay school board members sometimes even feel that special services are a waste of money because nothing can be done for children who are born dull and will always remain dull. We now know differently and new approaches have been developed, so this attitude will have to change. In the meantime, however, thousands of parents find themselves in a situation where special services are not available. Because of this I am writing this guide to what parents themselves can do to help their children.

Should parents teach their children?

Most parents are keenly aware of the problems which can arise in teaching their own children. It is hard to stand by and do nothing when the child needs help. Yet some teachers discourage parents from attempting any teaching at home. The parent naturally wonders what to do for the best.

The answer depends upon your personality, and upon the extent to which you are able to train yourself to be a good teacher of your child. Some parents are lucky enough to have just the right temperament, so that they are naturally good teachers. In a small remedial reading group of slow-learning children who came to me with their parents on Saturday mornings several years ago I had a father like this. He brought along his eleven-year-old son, who had been referred for testing within a few weeks of his starting school at the age of five because of his extreme unresponsiveness. Since he did not respond in the testing situation either, he was diagnosed as mentally retarded and excluded from school. He spent the next six years in an Occupational Centre where no attempt was made to teach him to read. My observation of him showed that he suffered from a severe handicap of temperament. He was so apprehensive about anything strange or supposedly difficult that he shrank from answering. Even though we could see that he knew, he would be afraid to commit himself until he received an encouraging nod. From the beginning his father showed admirable understanding and patience with him. Over the next year and a half he attended regularly each Saturday, learned how to play each game of the Programmed Reading Kit,[2] took home the materials and played with his son during the week. The boy made steady progress. It was evident that he had normal mental ability, which up to then he was too uncertain of himself to use. He became a good reader, and subsequently mastered elementary arithmetic without difficulty. At this stage, when he was thirteen, his father applied to have him re-admitted to school, and he was re-tested. Evidently his apprehensiveness took control of him in the

2. See the descriptions of the learning games in Appendix.

test-situation, and he was once again given a low IQ. In view of this it was decided that he was still "ineducable" and once again denied the opportunity of going to school.

How some parents can teach their children was borne in upon me a little time back when a teacher in a school for the trainable retarded told me she had a "mongoloid" boy who could read. I gave him some reading material that he had not seen before, and he read it slowly but surely. His reading level was that of the average eight-year-old child, one year above his age! His mother had taught him to read—how she had done so I was not able to find out, but she must have been a very good natural teacher.

In contrast, one finds parents who are sensible in everything else, but their anxiety makes it difficult for them to teach their own children. One of the best teachers in our Centre once brought in her three-year-old son so that we could try out some of our new learning games for young children. Although she showed great skill and patience with other young children, she prodded her own child anxiously. When I quietly remarked, "You're being a mother now, not a teacher," she laughed in recognition and began to use her teacher skills. The chief danger in parents' teaching their children is that out of anxiety they get too involved, press the child too hard and may even get angry with him. Untrained parents often assume that teaching is merely a matter of telling the child something and expecting him to remember it. When this doesn't succeed they think the child is being stubborn.

A broad truism which should guide the parent's

efforts is that the learning-situation should be a happy one. The child will then want to repeat it time and again. If, on the other hand, learning is associated with being forced, having to sit still for a long time and continually being expected to face difficult problems, then the child will be unable to give his whole mind to the task. It is not that he is being awkward or obstinate, although it looks that way. Unconsciously he is avoiding an unpleasant activity. This avoidance is beyond the control of his will. Although he may desperately want to attend, his mind wanders to other thoughts, or is blocked by fear of failure. The result is that he gives random answers, getting wrong what he shortly before had right.

Very few people can face tasks that they are not confident of being able to perform. If you doubt this, ask yourself when you last tried to do something without knowing if you would succeed or not. You will find on thinking about them that the jobs you dislike are those which contain an element of uncertainty, where there is a chance—even though quite a small one—of things going wrong. Perhaps it is ironing a collar that might crease or wrinkle, or putting a washer on a tap not knowing whether you can make it fit. Despite the assurances of expert do-it-yourself paper hangers that the job is easy, few of us are willing to risk it, because it looks difficult. With these thoughts in mind we can imagine the tensions which a child must feel in having to produce answers in an unfamiliar and probably difficult task which is not of his own choosing. In extreme cases children develop pains or feel sick or dizzy as a means of avoiding the task. There is no reason to think that they don't really feel ill, since the mechanism of avoidance works below the level of consciousness and can produce pains and feelings of sickness when required.

2

Training the parent
to be a good teacher

Overcoming parental anxiety

Do we have to accept it as a rule that the anxious parent should not try to teach his or her child? Since the majority of parents will feel anxiety about the failure of their children to progress, and their anxiety, if not controlled, will probably make them poor teachers, it is tempting to say that most parents should leave the education of their children to other people.

When, at our Centre, we notice a child having some special difficulty, we make an analysis of what seems to be wrong and design a means of overcoming it. The problem of the parent's anxiety in teaching his or her own child can be analysed in the same way. It is then a question, as with the bad learning habits of a child, of devising a programme by which the parent is made aware of his or her faults and learns good methods of teaching. It is a form of what psychologists call behaviour modification. With the children in our Centre we build the learning into a game. The

PARENT-AS-TEACHER SELF-RATING SCALE

Child's attitude to beginning the game:

Dates of "lessons"

Asked to play; reminded you it was time, accepted eagerly.	+2
Accepted with good grace.	+1
Was reluctant but agreed on promise of reward.	- 1
Tried to refuse, but you browbeat him into it.	- 2
You usually get a + score, but he didn't want to play today and you didn't press.	+1

When he made a mistake:

You said nothing and gave no sign of disappointment, but let the activity itself teach him.	+2
You suggested he could have another try.	+1
You say it is wrong when he can see this himself.	- 1
You told him he could do it if he tried, pointed out he didn't look properly or think it out. You often remind him to be careful, look well, think first.	- 2

When he hesitated, faltered or lost confidence:

You prodded him, told him to hurry up, he must learn to make up his mind, etc.	- 2
You just showed him the answer.	- 1

You nodded in encouragement when he was on the right track and he waited for your cue.	+1								
You varied the problem to make it easier, but left him to find the final answer.	+2								

When he got the right answer:

You said, "There, you can do it when you try (think, look, etc.)".	- 2								
You got ambitious to see if he could manage something harder.	- 1								
You said nothing but an occasional "that's right" etc.	+1								
You praised or expressed pleased surprise (without overdoing it).	+2								

How the game finished:

On a happy note with intention of resuming tomorrow.	+2								
Began to show signs of genuine fatigue, or lack of interest.	+1								
Wanted to stop, but you used devices to keep game going.	- 1								
You made him continue against his will.	- 2								
Total score for day									

Separate copies of this form can be obtained from the publisher of this book for use with a group of parents or to distribute to a parents' meeting. It would, however, be no breach of copyright for you to make a copy of it for your own use.   © D.H. Stott 1971

13

correct behaviour brings success, and the child is pleased. This makes him more inclined to use the same approach next time, until he establishes a good learning habit.

The Parent-as-Teacher Self-rating Scale Following the same principles, you as a parent can play a kind of game with yourself in which you can assess your own teaching behaviour. It consists of making an entry, after each learning session with your child, on the Parent-as-Teacher Self-Rating Scale, a small replica of which is reproduced here. For each of the five stages you give yourself a plus or minus rating according to the way you react and the effect on your child. You must not blame yourself if at first you get minus marks for some stages. The way your child responds may be the result of previous wrong attitudes on your part or the distaste for learning that he has developed owing to his failure in school. The important thing is that over the weeks you should improve your score. By the time you are getting 7's or 8's (or more) you can be sure that you have created a happy learning situation for your child and that you have become a good teacher. Let us take each of the five stages and discuss them in turn.

The child's attitude to beginning the game

You should plan very carefully how you introduce the learning games. Best of all ask your child if he has a friend whom he would like to invite home to play table games. It may be advisable to start with a well-

14

known game like Concentration or Fish, or the more educational versions of these games described in the Appendix. Do not start with an active runabout game like pingpong or table hockey, for if he is a hyperactive child he may want to stay with this type of activity. Something will be gained if he and his pal learn to sit quietly at a table. This does not mean that they will have to be inactive. All the games recommended allow for quite a bit of bodily movement. This takes care of the child's fidgets and prevents boredom.

Your child may be so unorganized in his behaviour that he cannot take turns in a game with another child. He lacks patience at a time when he wants badly to make a move or place a piece, and so he goes ahead out of turn or yells at his partner to hurry up. In the Flying Start Learning-to-Learn Kit[1] there is a game—the Merry-Go-Rounds—invented in order to train children like this. Each player has the alternate parts of a circle, which only fit together to make pictures when placed next to one of the other player's pieces. Thus, after placing one piece, each player has to wait for the other to place his. The fun consists in completing the circle, which is a visible form of achievement. We had the gratification of finding that this game worked better than we had anticipated. Even some hyperactive children who would not bother with any of the other games became intrigued with the making of the circle. Then they became interested in the other learning games.

1. All the games and materials referred to throughout this book are described in the Appendix.

It may be that, at the beginning, you have to act as play partner to your child yourself, either because he is not yet ready to play with another child or because there are none available. If this is the situation make sure that you do not always win. With a young child you should occasionally make a mistake and say something like, "Well I never! I couldn't have been looking properly" or "I didn't give myself time to think it out".

At first you may have to cope with a reluctance on the part of your child to play the games. This may be because he has already developed an over-active style of behaviour, or because he prefers to do something else. Naturally you should not try to drag him away from some other play that he is enjoying. You may have to wait a week or two, until the phase is past or the weather changes. There are very few children who can find a constant succession of activities for themselves, so wait for a period of "don't know what to do".

Having persuaded him to give the game a trial it is important that he retain a pleasant memory of it for next time. After a few times he may be giving you plus marks by asking to play or reminding you that it is play hour. This theme of making the learning game enjoyable runs through all the five stages, but there are a few general principles which we can consider here. First, a child normally appreciates the attention and companionship of an adult, provided the adult does not adopt an overbearing attitude. So show yourself ready to participate and make up your mind to enjoy the occasion yourself. If he asks you to play at a time when you are busy try not to refuse outright, but tell him to get out the pieces and then drop along to take your turn at moments when you are free. If this cannot be managed, suggest that you play later when the other parent can see how well he is doing and/or suggest he has a try at making one of the puzzles for you.

The game can be made more pleasurable by the anticipation of some treat. It is permissible to associate the game with eating or drinking something special. But produce the goodies unpromised and unannounced after a spell of enjoyable play. He will then learn to link them in his mind with his good play behaviour and be more likely to play well next time. Do not get into a bargaining situation with him or try to cajole him into playing with promises of treats. If you do, you will train him to manipulate you, to make more and more demands of the wrong type, and to throw a temper tantrum when you have to refuse.

It is well to remember that children's interests come and go in phases. Just as he will get a craze for playing, say, Cowboys and Indians, for a couple of weeks and then tire of it, so he may well decide that he wants a change from the learning games. If he has played willingly for a few days and then one day says he doesn't want to play, you should accept this and let the games rest for a time.

When he made a mistake

The single important thing to remember is that experience is the best teacher. All the learning games recommended are so planned that to win at them consistently the child has to use a good technique. He has to look carefully and think before he acts. If he doesn't take the trouble to look properly, or if he guesses, he will quickly see that in that way he will never succeed. The game itself will teach him good learning habits. There is thus no point in your constantly pointing out his faults to him. This will only be harmful. No one likes to have attention drawn to his faults, and if you yield to the temptation to rub his in, you create an unpleasant situation. The result may well be that, far from correcting his faulty behaviour, he gets turned off the game altogether. You will have broken the first rule: that playing the games must be an enjoyable occasion.

The only exception to this 'no nagging' rule is when you can make a bit of fun or make-believe out of the child's mannerisms. I observed how a mother did this with her extremely hyperactive son who seemed incapable of keeping his feet still while sitting at a table. The constant swinging of his feet was in fact distracting him from the game. On one occasion she said to him something like this, "I've found a good way of winning. When I want to think which card to take I keep my feet still". He tried it and it worked! From then on there was a marked improvement in his play habits. A few days later, when the mother made one of her intentional mistakes, he exclaimed: "Mummy, you did not keep your feet still".

If the child makes a mistake, say nothing for a while. You must not give the impression that every one of his moves is being checked. It does not matter if a wrong move is overlooked for the moment, because it will become apparent later in the game. If it is necessary eventually to draw his attention to it, try saying, "Something must have gone wrong here. Let's take this piece off and see if we can fit it in a better place".

When he hesitated, faltered or lost confidence

The worst thing to do in these circumstances is of course to show your anxiety or impatience by telling him to hurry up. Lack of confidence and over-sensitivity about failure take an extreme form in some children and constitute a severe learning handicap if they are treated in the wrong way. This handicap of temperament can cause a child to be diagnosed as retarded, and since he will "freeze" in the test situation just as he does before everything else that is unfamiliar, the false diagnosis will be confirmed by a low IQ.

With this sort of child, whom we describe as "unforthcoming", there is also danger of the opposite kind. If the child shrinks from giving an answer and then finds that the adult tells him, he may realize that he only has to appear "dumb" and the pressure is off. The more stupid he seems to be, the less people will expect of him. He retreats into the safe refuge of dependency and retardation. Naturally he is also clever enough to oblige with a low IQ.

The documentary film "Learning to learn"[2] shows a five-year-old girl who quite obviously is being as

2. This film can be bought or rented. For particulars write to Audio Visual, University of Guelph, Guelph, Ontario.

stupid as she can think how to be. When she happens to put two pieces of a puzzle together correctly she takes them apart to make them wrong. When making the film, I called her bluff by telling her I knew she was just teasing us all the time. From that point on she decided to learn. In the next film, "Johnny can learn to read",[3] she is seen making the sounds of the letters and fusing them to make simple words. At each of her successes she nods her head as if to say, "That's another one right!" We were fortunate in catching her when she was just flirting with retardation as a way of life.

With the unforthcoming child both teacher and parent have to learn to steer a fine course between arousing his apprehensions and letting him give up trying. If he is pressured—or even put in a position where he feels himself called upon to give answers—his mind will be completely taken up with the awful fear of failure, so that he just cannot attend to the problem. If, on the other hand, everything is done for him and he is protected against any challenge, his mind will remain undeveloped and he will become retarded in fact. His basic handicap is that he assumes he cannot cope. The solution is to train—or as psychologists would say—condition him to develop an attitude of "I can do it". This training must follow well-defined rules. At first he should be given tasks which are really too easy for him, and he should be praised when he carries them out correctly. Even after he has shown that he can do tasks of a certain

3. This film can be bought or rented. For particulars write to Audio Visual, University of Guelph, Guelph, Ontario.

kind without difficulty he should be allowed to do still more of them. Each stage should build on the previous one, in such a way that his feeling of confidence can be extended to the new task. There should be only a very small advance in difficulty, so that he makes progress without his apprehensions being aroused.

Of course this is an ideal to aim at; it would be impossible to plan the child's learning programme so that he never loses confidence. It is on these occasions that we have to know how to get him out of a situation which will reinforce his sense of failure. We have seen that it is fatal to prod him. On the other hand it may be equally dangerous to tell him the answer every time he looks to the parent or teacher for a cue. It is much better to vary the problem to make it easier. It may even be necessary to make the solution quite obvious. But the final act of solving the problem must always be left to the child, so that he gets the feeling that he has solved it by his own efforts.

Unforthcoming children often become very skillful at getting adults to tell them the answers. They half say something or move their hand towards a card, and wait until they get an encouraging signal. If the signal doesn't come, they assume they are wrong and try their luck with another answer. This is obviously not an effective method of learning. Nevertheless it is very difficult to refrain from giving an encouraging nod or uttering an encouraging murmur. There are two ways out of the dilemma. The first is to build up the child's confidence in the ways described above, so that he has less need to depend upon other people for answers. The second is to take the first opportunity of finding a play partner for your child, and for you to slip into the background.

When he got the right answer

When things are going well there are only two dangers. The first is to avoid tarnishing the rewards of success by any kind of moralizing, pointing the lesson or referring to episodes of contrariness or failure, such as "Why can't you always be like this?" or "You see how well you can do when you try".

The second danger is to let your ambition on the child's behalf run away with you. When he has succeeded in something for the first time it is terribly hard not to get over-optimistic, and try to get him to do the next stage also. If you yield to this temptation you will soon come to the point where he fails. You will then be depriving him of the enjoyment of his recent accomplishment. In the mastery of new activities the average child goes through a cycle. At the experimental stage he is very cautious, often trying the task as if accidentally, so that if he fails he can pretend he was not really trying to do anything in particular. Once he sees that it works he feels he can commit himself, and does it time and time again with evident glee. Finally, when he gets so that it becomes too easy and he gets no "kick" out of it, he drops it and looks around for something else. So let him exploit his success to the fullest without hurrying him on to the next stage. During this time of successful accomplishment he will be strengthening his feeling of being able to cope. This is the memory that you wish him to carry over to the next time. If you

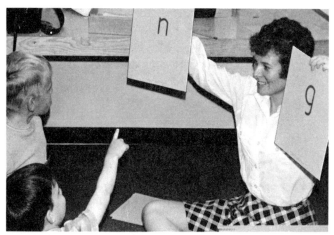

A student (above) and a volunteer mother (below) using the Giant Touch Cards with Kindergarten children who were referred to the Centre because of learning disabilities.

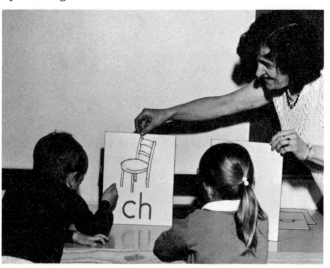

push him on prematurely to the next stage the session will end on a note of failure, and he will be less eager to begin the next one. The rule is, therefore, that when the child has made one gain let him make the most of it for a time.

How the game finished

Your success in keeping the parent-as-teacher programme going will depend in large part on whether each session ends happily. You will therefore have to be firm with yourself about how long you keep the learning game going. It is best of all to stop before the child's interest and attention begin to flag. In any event, stop immediately you begin to see this happening.

Sometimes you may feel that you have accomplished little, because for most of the learning time you had to agree to play some game of his own choosing. But you will have laid the foundations for future successful work with him; at the very least you have done something to establish a ritual of playing a game together at a certain time each day.

How much compulsion should a parent use? Often you may get exasperated, suspecting that your child is being lazy, pretending to be stupid or tired or not well, or that he is taking advantage of your "softness". Of course children are tempted to play up in these ways. This can also happen at school when a child feels he is failing, and the teacher cannot give in to it. You may ask why I propose a different method of handling the child at school compared with at home. At school a child expects to do learning tasks and accepts the fact that the teacher is there to see that he does them. But he does not view his home or you as his parents in that way. After a day in school, home should be a place of relative freedom and relaxation. I am not implying that it is all right for school to be an unpleasant place. Learning there should be enjoyable just as it is in the home. Nevertheless, because of his or her accepted professional role, the teacher has greater scope than the parent for dealing with a child's attempts to avoid work.

For the parent to use any sort of compulsion in getting the child to learn at home is altogether too great a risk. The consequences of it may spread to the child's learning in school, and the teacher will have just cause to complain. Every experienced teacher of the early grades can recognize the parental-pressure syndrome. The child approaches the task with obvious tension, gives anxious half-thought-out answers which are little better than guesses, often goes "blank" so that he cannot give an answer that he gave a moment before and seems to suffer from a failure of memory.

In short, if you cannot persuade your child to play the learning games willingly or at least with gracious consent, you should not try to make him do so. If, soon after he has begun, he says he doesn't want to go on, you should acquiesce. If he is willing to play some other game of his choice, go along with him in this. He may well, out of a sense of fairness, play the game you want to play next time. The best tactic of all, if it can be managed, is for a small group of parents to arrange to play the learning games once a week with their children, say, on Saturday morning in each of their homes in turn. The occasion will naturally be made a bit of a party, with drinks and cookies. The unwilling child should be allowed to attend without any condition that he take part in the games. He should even be allowed to bring along his own toy. Very few children can refrain from joining in a game which they see others enjoying. The chances are, therefore, that before long he will join in spontaneously.

If he disrupts the game or refuses to play properly you should not get angry with him, but suggest that he play with his own toys until he feels he can play as the other children do. He should be allowed to return to the game as soon as he likes, and be accepted in the same matter-of-fact way as is an adult who leaves a card game for a while to prepare some refreshments. You should be especially careful not to say that he can join in again if he is a good boy, or mention the particular fault which caused his exclusion. He must be allowed to return without losing face.

Rating yourself as parent-teacher It is one thing to read a lot of good advice; it is quite another thing to bear it constantly in mind when you begin to get emotionally involved in a situation. So you will have to give yourself a period of training as a parent-teacher. This means reviewing your performance after each session. As a means of organizing this you should use the Parent-as-Teacher Rating Scale.

After each play-learning time with your child give yourself a score of from plus two to minus two for each of the five sections. When you have to give yourself a minus score for any of them, this will remind you not to repeat the same fault next time. As mentioned earlier, your score will depend in part upon the general relationship you are able to build up with your child and his willingness to play the games. Consequently your score at any one time is a measure of your general progress as well as how well you did at the last session.

We wish progressively to improve this Rating Scale, and thereby to improve our techniques of training parents to act as teachers. Consequently we should be glad to hear accounts from you of awkward situations to which it does not seem to provide the answer.

3

"Intelligence"

Ask the man-in-the-street why some children do well in school and others not. He will tell you "We can't all be clever", or "We can't all have the brains". A young man who never did well may come to terms with his poor attainment by saying, "I was one of the stupid ones". The idea that everybody is born with so much of a mysterious essence or quality called "intelligence" is ingrained in our society. Psychologists have adopted the idea and made it look scientifically respectable by inventing and using intelligence tests. They point to the undoubted fact that the students who do well at school are usually those who have high IQ's. The trouble about this neat explanation of academic success and failure is that there are too many exceptions. Many parents who have written to me point out that their learning-disabled child is quite bright in other matters. I believe them, because many of the illiterate youths I have known and worked with were not unintelligent in real life. What is more, some children with very low IQ's are good readers. If one person with supposedly very little intelligence can learn to read we are entitled to ask why others cannot also. Then there are the numerous poor readers and non-readers whose IQ's indicate average or superior intelligence.

The basic weakness of explanations in terms of intelligence is that, quite literally, we don't know what we are talking about. Psychologists have not been able to agree about what intelligence is. To say that it is the ability to perform academic tasks such as dealing with theories or abstractions is to argue in a circle, because this is the ability that we are trying to explain. At this point I can hear many of my readers exclaim, "Anyone can see that some people are more intelligent than others! What about all those brilliant scientists, or mathematicians, or poets? What about Shakespeare, or Darwin?"

Let us pause to consider the kinds of facts we are dealing with. It is true that some people can function mentally at a much higher level than others. We can agree that they *behave* more intelligently when faced with a problem. But need we attribute this to some essence called "intelligence"? If we did, the chemist or the physicist might challenge us by saying, "How do you observe intelligence? All your observations have to do with behaviour and skills, and there may be many reasons why some people become highly skilled at those tasks which you use as measures of intelligence." And these scientists would be right. The notion of intelligence is by no means scientifically respectable. All we are measuring is a person's behaviour in a problem-solving situation.

And yet nearly all teachers and practically everyone

29

THE PARENT AS TEACHER

else takes the reality of intelligence for granted. The famous Australian archaeologist, Sir Leonard Woolley, from his observations of the ways of thought of many civilizations ancient and modern, wrote that there is no limit to the silly things that people can think, provided everybody thinks them. Leaving aside the issue of intelligence for a while, let us review a "silly" idea that learned men accepted for thousands of years as a self-evident truth. I am referring to the ancient way of explaining differences in people's temperaments: that every person contained a mixture of what were considered the four basic elements—earth, fire, air, water; the proportions within each individual determined his temperament. To us, now, this is a primitive, pre-scientific notion. But let us imagine that we could transport ourselves back, say, four hundred years, and drop in to a seminar given by a famous professor of the Renaissance on this very theory. After a while one of us gets impatient, and interrupts him with the question, "What evidence is there that people have so much earth, fire, air and water inside them?"

We can picture the incredulous look on the face of the professor at being asked what seems to him such a stupid question. He might turn to his students and ask rhetorically, "Don't we all know people with fiery temperaments? Can't you see the heat coming out of them? Aren't there people who are airy and flighty, whom you can't pin down to a sensible argument? And what about those stolid fellows whose temperaments are heavy with all the earth they have in them? Or the people who flow this way and that like water, following the latest fashion and easily influenced by any persuasive tongue? We know that all matter is composed of earth, fire, air and water. We human beings are matter. Isn't it obvious," he would say, clinching the argument, "that the differences we see in people's temperaments are due to the different amounts they contain of these fundamental elements?" Yes, it is obvious, his class would agree with him, eyeing the ignorant intruder who could thus fly in the face of facts.

Where did that professor of the Renaissance go wrong in his reasoning? His observations about people's temperaments were acute enough, but from a scientific point of view he took a fatal false step. He assumed that the individual differences were due to the presence of substances about which he had no direct evidence. In a hundred years time I am sure that people who think in terms of an essence or quality which we call intelligence will be regarded as just as quaint and primitive in their thinking as we now regard the Renaissance professor and his students. Perhaps we shall have made this advance in twenty years time. Who knows? Speaking to school psychologists along these lines I find them surprisingly ready to go along with me. Perhaps the turn in our thinking is just round the corner.

I have taken up so much space with this apparently academic discussion of intelligence because you as a parent must not get overawed by such notions, and may even have to argue with educators against the so-called evidence of an IQ.

You may feel that you are not equipped with enough knowledge to sustain such an argument. Suppose, for example, that someone who still believes in intelligence retorts, "Surely the differences in people's mental ability are obvious. Indeed, we can measure them".

Look at how
they learn
You need not give up at this point, because there is a great deal of evidence lying at hand which he has overlooked. He has only been looking for one thing—success or failure in a test—which constantly bolsters up his notion of intelligence. But let us take him into a class of young children and observe how they set about learning. We see that a great many of them are busily engaged in constructing, or drawing, or dressing up and having a make-believe dinner party, or pulling something to pieces to see how it works, or studying thoughtfully the pictures in a book. These children are developing their minds. From their experience they are getting a lot of information about the things around them and the world at large. They try to do something first this way, then that, and note the method that works. They remember the ways of tackling problems that were successful, and try them again. They get the idea that if you take the time to work something out, you will probably be able to do so.

Children get considerable satisfaction from seeing in the street objects that they have seen in pictures, and vice versa. They watch their parents making purchases, and note that so much of each commodity is bought and that a certain quantity of money has to be paid for it, and then they play games with each other or with their dolls, asking for so many eggs, so much money, etc. Because of their active curiosity and reflectiveness they come to understand ideas such as those of quantity and number. They listen to adults speaking, wonder about some unknown word they overhear, and decide what it must mean. Then they mouth it to themselves, and eventually begin to use it.

In short, these are the children who are likely to do well over the years in school. They will become skillful at solving complex problems because they have the knowledge, and they have arranged it in nice little packages which are readily available for use when required. Moreover, they approach every new problem with the confidence that they will solve it, or at least learn something interesting in trying to do so. They are regarded as intelligent children. When it comes to doing a so-called intelligence test their problem-solving skills stand them in good stead, and they get high IQ's.

The pattern of inconsequence

Let us return to our Kindergarten or Pre-school and observe another child, one likely to be a slow learner. He is physically much more active. At the moment we appear he is racing around the room on a tricycle, perhaps bumping into objects and laughing, or mischievously riding over some other child's construction. When the teacher restrains him and suggests he might like to build a house with some wooden blocks, he throws them around the room, chases after them and throws them again. Then he picks up a toy broom and starts banging against a wall. Happening to displace a child's drawing that has been pinned there, he begins to sweep the other drawings off also, with great energy and evident satisfaction. Finally he swings the broom violently in the air without looking, and hits another child. The next week he doesn't come to school. His mother phones to explain that he jumped out of the car before it stopped, fell out and cut himself badly. The nursery school teacher suppresses an unworthy exclamation of relief.

Children of this type—we call them inconsequent because they do not check on the consequences of their actions—learn certain things because they are alert and always ready to experiment. But their experimentation is of a thoughtless, trial-and-error type. They never give themselves time to think. Even if they have learned something, they don't bring their knowledge to bear on the task because they act too impetuously. When faced with a problem which needs a little reflection they merely guess.

What is fundamentally wrong with these children? It is that they cannot control their impulses: they act in the first way that comes into their heads. They do the same during a so-called intelligence test. Because they respond eagerly, even though at random, they get a certain score, but their IQ's will usually be rated as "low-average" or "dull-average"—meaning something in the range of 85 to 90. Their parents know that they can be quite smart, especially in their quick repartee and their dodges to get out of things.

Can we then say that the inconsequent child is unintelligent? The fact is that, even if we think along these lines, we have no means of finding out. He is not setting his brain to work on problems, whether these be in his daily life, in academic tasks or in an intelligence test. He by-passes—short-circuits—the

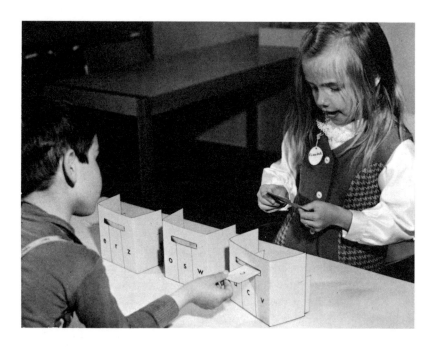

The Mail Boxes train children in attention and in taking the time to look carefully. One child posts the letters in the boxes while the other checks to see if the half-pictures on their reverse sides fit the halves on the floor of the box.

thinking parts of his brain because he acts before they have time to function.

Very soon he finds that his habit of making quick guesses doesn't work with certain kinds of problems. This applies particularly to anything complex, such as learning to read or doing arithmetic. He becomes discouraged and gives up. From this point on he uses his brains to avoid academic tasks, and becomes very skillful in doing so. He is likely also to compensate for his failure by making the most of activities by which he can create some effect—gross physical movement, rough-and-tumble games, playing the clown. Some such children discover the satisfactions of annoying people and become nuisances. Their life degenerates into a constant war with their teachers. Little wonder they cannot learn. A diagnosis of their disability in terms of intelligence is wide of the mark. The quality of their brains is irrelevant because they are not using the parts of them that could make their behaviour intelligent.

The pattern of unforthcomingness Returning to our imaginary Preschool we next observe a child whose behaviour is the very opposite of that of the boisterous inconsequent. She—for this type of child is more likely to be a girl—is extremely shy, creeps into a quiet corner away from other children, does not seem to notice what they are doing and ignores most of the toys. If you as a stranger ask her a question the chances are that she will not answer at all. She keeps her dealings with the world down to the very minimum. We call her type the unforthcoming child. Her basic handicap is an extreme apprehensiveness in the face of anything unfamiliar or what she imagines to be difficult. She assumes that any task she is asked to perform will be beyond her. She has a great fear of displeasing by giving the wrong answer, and so—when asked anything—she just freezes ("withdraws into her shell" as teachers say of her), or at best looks for an encouraging nod before she finally commits herself. In Chapter Two there is a fairly detailed picture of how she behaves in a learning situation, including the defence she may put up of being dull so that she is no longer subjected to the anxiety of being pushed into situations where she has to give answers. In pre-school or Kindergarten she exploits this strategy of withdrawal to good effect. She is what teachers think of as a dull child. At home her parents will know her as unventuresome. She may prefer to stay at home to play rather than meet the other children on the street, and may need a lot of prompting to go alone to a corner store. But they will never have thought of her as stupid. Rather they will see her as a reliable, sensible child who is competent at the household jobs she undertakes.

When she is tested they are surprised and disappointed to learn that she has a low IQ and hence—so the logic of intelligence goes—can never be expected to achieve much in school. The truth is that in the test she developed the same apprehensiveness, and used the same tactics of freezing, as she uses in school or in a social situation. After all, the tasks set in an intelligence test have been designed to be unfamiliar because they are meant to exclude the influence of previous learning. Thus they are just the

THE PARENT AS TEACHER

sort of problem that frightens the unforthcoming child and produces no response from her. The resulting IQ is merely a measure of her handicap of temperament.

Unfortunately the problem is not just a matter of a child's response during the testing. For years the inconsequent child has resorted to guessing rather than thinking out solutions. The unforthcoming child has fought shy of the problems themselves. Neither has gained any experience of how to tackle tasks that need thought. Neither has given much study to the nature of the things around them. Their minds remain unskilled and unstocked. Even if their wrong approach to learning were suddenly remedied, and they tried their very best to solve problems, whether in an intelligence test or otherwise, they would be ill-equipped to do so. Mentally, they have no pegs to hang things on. Thus, eventually, they become, to all practical purposes, backward or retarded.

4

About maladjustment

A little knowledge is a helpful thing How successful you are in teaching your child will depend in large part upon your general relationship with him. You cannot expect to be able to "turn on" good attitudes during the teaching hour if at every other time you feel frustrated, angry, or guilty in your child's presence. If you don't understand why he should be so difficult, or lacking in go, while your friends' children are happy and alert and seldom need correction, you will be tempted to write him off as the black sheep, or the dunce, of the family. If you cannot understand why your efforts to discipline or stimulate him meet with no success you may take it out on him rather than admit you are failing as a parent. Helplessness can breed rejection. If your ego is threatened you are likely to panic into attack or flight. Losing control of your emotions, you will be unable to plan any strategies, and may as well give up reading this book.

It is therefore important for you to have some

understanding, in the first place, of how your child's temperamental handicap arose—at least to the extent that you no longer fall into a state of despondent self-blame. Once you have this understanding your attitude to your child will improve, probably without your realizing it. The same happens to teachers when, say, as a result of being asked to report objectively on students' undesirable behaviour, they come to realize that they may be dealing with symptoms of maladjustment. Then they no longer feel it as a threat to their professional competence or as wilfulness that must be dealt with severely. Rather they see the student as needing their help. The student, sensing the more sympathetic attitude, feels better towards the teacher and his behaviour improves. In the following chapters I am therefore going to discuss what we know about the origins of the relatively common types of maladjustment so that you as a parent may also be able to replace your annoyance or disappointment with the realization that you have to help your child overcome his handicap.

Secondly, to reduce your feelings of helplessness and to save you from the errors of blind attack or avoidance, I am going to make some suggestions about how you may learn to manage the handicap. Naturally, I do not presume to be able to usurp the function of the therapist. But from my experience of how calamities have happened I can list a small number of things to do and not to do, which apply to all parents and children because they are human beings with human needs.

The origins of behaviour disturbance Psychologists are not yet agreed upon the origins of behaviour disturbances. The view handed down to us by our forefathers was that each of us was born with a number of character traits, some good, some bad. Scientists of the latter part of the nineteenth century, and well into the twentieth, were convinced, as good Darwinians, that all the chief differences between individuals were inherited. It followed that some people were born of bad, and even criminal stock and consequently would grow up bad or criminal. Even today the idea still lingers that a "black sheep" can turn up in any family, and I have heard both parents and teachers express the opinion that some children are "just wicked". We cannot dismiss the idea that some types of abnormal behaviour are inherited, and indeed there is some evidence that this is so. But we are really dealing with temperamental handicaps which may be regarded as "bad behaviour" because of their effect upon us. A handicap may be inherited, but not "badness".

During the 1930's and the 1940's there was a strong swing towards an environmental view. How a child turned out was attributed entirely to the influences brought to bear on him. Chief among these was the stability and quality of the affection he received from his mother. It followed that if the mother had had the care of him in his early years, and he became maladjusted, she was to blame.

I remember, many years ago, a member of a profession who should have known better saying to the press in reference to a college student who had committed suicide, that he must have suffered emotional deprivation in early childhood. This was not only a cruel thing to say, but there is no scientific support for this automatic connection between maladjustment and faulty early mothering.

This myth of early deprivation has become so ingrained in our culture that mothers have come to me full of guilt because they allowed their child to go into hospital for a week; and demands have been made that hospitals should take the mother into hospital with the child. I have published a study which shows that some children can be separated for years from their mothers without bad effects[1]. This and another well-known study[2] show that the way in which the child is treated in the home at the present time is more important than what happened to him years ago. If, therefore, you have a maladjusted child, you should ask yourself what you may be doing wrong now, not how you might have failed him in infancy.

Of course the way a child is brought up can be a handicap to him. He may never have learned to mind his p's and q's, which—in the language of the psychologist—means a lack of social learning. He may have been spoiled, that is to say, he has been conditioned to believe that his wishes are the only ones that count, and his egotism and lack of realism may dog

1. D.H. Stott, "The effects of separation from the mother in early life," Lancet, May 5, 1966.
2. Hilda Lewis, *Deprived Children*, Oxford University Press, 1954.

him throughout his life. If he has been deprived of the security of a reliable family base he will—as I shall point out later—be subject to anxiety and hostility.

Despite these not inconsiderable effects of upbringing, the fact remains that stable, sensible children are found in circumstances that one would think should make any child maladjusted. And some extremely disturbed children have parents whom one has to rate not only as stable and affectionate, but as having shown almost superhuman patience and tolerance. Parents who have been careful to give each of their children equal affection and consideration find that their temperaments are totally different—and they were so from birth! We have to ask why—as so often happens—there should be just one problem child in a family in which the other children are all well-adjusted.[3] We cannot dismiss the idea that some children are born with handicaps of temperament.

3. D.H. Stott, *Studies of Troublesome Children*. Toronto, Methuen Publications; New York, Humanities Press; London, Tavistock Publications, 1966.

5

The Inconsequent child

The origins of inconsequence

Inconsequence is a type of mal-adjustment often met in stable and well-to-do homes, and usually only one child in a family is affected. We can get a clue about the origin of the condition by how early in life the symptoms appeared. Many parents of an inconsequent child report abnormal symptoms, such as persistent crying, or hyperactivity, from babyhood. Others say that the problems date back only from about the age of two or three years, possibly following a severe virus infection or an accident. Nearly all mention some abnormality of development, such as delayed speech, poor motor coordination and habit disorders. In some thirty cases studied at our Centre for Educational Disabilities there was more than the usual degree of ill-health, and of events and circumstances calculated to produce severe emotional distress, during the mother's pregnancy. Another hint comes from statements which have often been made to me by parents. The father, now characteristically a successful businessman, may say, "I was just like that when I was young". Or the mother may tell of her brother who fitted the pattern, and has always remained irresponsible. Possibly, then, inconsequence runs in families. If the child has only one of the genes he may become an active, enterprising man. If he has both genes he may have "too much of a good thing" and spoil himself by his impulsiveness.

It must, however, be admitted that we have insufficient evidence to be positive about the origins of inconsequence. Such pointers as we have indicate that it is congenital—a term which means merely that it originates from birth or before birth. This does not mean that it is inherited, although it might be. To judge from what we know of many other congenital conditions, there could be an inherited tendency which is triggered off by some stressful conditions of the mother's pregnancy. The first of these pointers is that inconsequence is much more common among boys than among girls. In a large survey recently carried out among Ontario school-age students we found that over three times as many boys as girls met our criterion for inconsequence.

Some psychologists attribute all such sex differences to the different ways in which boys and girls are treated in their families—in this instance more aggressive behaviour being tolerated, or even encouraged, in males. However, the behaviour of an inconsequent child is not merely aggressive, and indeed may not be aggressive at all. Those who have observed his inability to settle down to a patient, thoughtful activity, his meddling and impulsive experimentation which so often lead to breakages and accidents, his tiresome pestering and attention-seeking, and his frequent inability to get on with other children, cannot in the least be inclined to condone or encourage his behaviour as emerging masculinity. The boot may be on the other foot: our concept of masculinity may be derived in part from the prevalence of inconsequence among us males. In sum, it looks as if more boys than girls are born with this maladjustment.

An even more telling pointer in the same direction is the tendency of inconsequent children to be sick more often than their well-adjusted fellows. In the above-mentioned survey the group who were rated as unhealthy (having three or more distinct health problems) contained nearly four times more children of the inconsequent type than the healthy group. This is an example of the Law of Multiple Impairment,[1] which states that if a child has one kind of handicap—whether it be physical, emotional or mental—he stands more than an equal chance of having a second; if he has two he has more than an equal chance of having a third, and so it goes on. It is hard to think of any reason for this link between many distinct handicaps except that they all go back to the same influences in the child's very early development—and most probably to birth or before.

Handling the inconsequent child   It is evident that, if my impressions and findings about the origins of inconsequence are borne out by research on a larger scale, the parents cannot be blamed if they have a child of this type. The important thing for you as the parent

1. D.H. Stott, *Studies of Troublesome Children*, ibid.

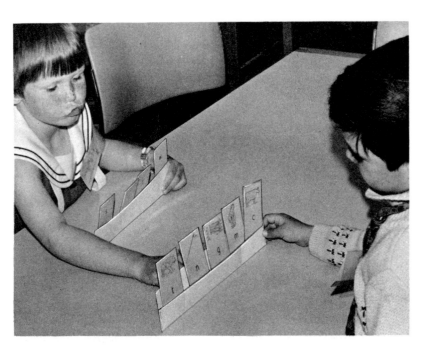

Two children play the Holder
Game with the Touch Cards.
Each in turn asks the other
where a picture is. The player
who is asked goes by the letter
on the reverse side of the card.
They win the cards only if they
choose right the first time. In
this way they learn not to guess.

is to know how best to handle him.

He may be sweet and good-natured, so that you and everyone else make allowances for him that a less charming child would not enjoy. Only his school reports, "lazy, is not doing his best, never does anything unless you stand over him", throw you periodically into despair. More commonly, the child gets on everyone's nerves by his incessant demands for attention, doing things in silly ways, squabbling with other children so that they avoid him, getting involved with others of his sort in crazy pranks. According to your temperament and training, you will be tempted either to try to cure him by harsh punishment, or to give up.

Punishment is effective only with the child who can "learn his lesson"—that is to say, who can attain sufficient control of himself to weigh the consequences of his acts in the light of his previous experience. These well-adjusted children learn quickly where their advantage lies and seldom require greater punishment than an expression of disapproval or the withdrawal of a privilege. I have known instances where inconsequent boys are frequently beaten by their fathers, who think that if only they beat them severely enough they are bound to mend their ways sometime. It does not have the desired effect. Even the floggings of the old-time army and navy could not have been all that effective, considering the frequent resort to execution as the ultimate solution. A harshly treated child builds up such strong resentments that these in themselves may become an overpowering motive. In the war between himself and his father he is prepared to risk the beatings provided he can score his points by becoming as unworthy a son as he knows how. He may also model himself on his father's treatment of him and become aggressive towards other children. Following one of my broadcasts a man wrote to me describing a childhood of this kind:

"I scarcely ever got any rewards but beatings and verbal abuse of every kind was continual with Dad and I took the defeatist attitude to school and didn't get along well there either especially with the other boys and girls.

"My brother is a qualified technologist and don't think was born with a better brain than me. But in my case Dad felt no need to restrain himself and the worse he treated the worse I was and the worse I was the worse he treated me. My brother was delicate in early childhood and Dad regretted that he couldn't lambast him the way he did me. So my brother grew up with confidence and competence I will never have and Dad admired him for it and didn't let me forget how much better he thought my brother did for his age than I did. I know I am a neurotic failure."

The other temptation, to give up, may take place insidiously and unconsciously. A father may arrange or choose his job or his recreations so that he is seldom at home with the child, leaving the problem with the mother. Some parents are able blandly to shut their eyes to their child's misbehaviour, pretending or convincing themselves that it is nothing out of the ordinary. He may then become an unholy terror in the neighbourhood, so that other parents forbid their children to play with him. To the inconsequence is added the licence to domineer and to be a nuisance.

One has to admit that there is no quick, magical

THE PARENT AS TEACHER

answer to the management of the inconsequent child. For years you have to strike a fine balance between insistence that he learn to control himself, and harsh punishment which will bring resentment in its train. You have constantly to fight the natural tendency, in any unpleasant situation, either to attack or to avoid rather than follow a considered strategy. The latter needs much self-training in patience. To this end you can cultivate two aids.

The first is to purge yourself of the old-fashioned eye-for-an-eye attitude to punishment by bearing in mind that your child suffers from a real handicap. He finds it much more difficult than other children to control his impulses. This realization will enable you not to get too emotionally involved. You will no longer feel that his misbehaviour is an insult and a challenge to you personally, against which you have to react in order to maintain your authority and self-respect. You can begin to train yourself as a therapist by viewing the child's progress more objectively. Train yourself to note what responses on your part cause an improvement or a worsening of his behaviour.

The second aid to patience is to realize that, although it will be a long haul, time is on your side. I said above that the inconsequent child finds it difficult to control his impulses. This is not to say that he cannot. He is hard to condition, but it can be done. The psychologist will point out that this requires a very consistent training schedule in which the desirable behaviour is inevitably rewarded and the undesirable behaviour inevitably "punished". By punishment the psychologist does not imply physical punishment or any intensely disagreeable treatment, but rather a course of action giving the child to understand that he is not gaining by his bad behaviour.

The conditioning process   What is being proposed, in short, is a form of behaviour modification. First let us consider what forms this behaviour modification should not take. I have already pointed out the dangers of physical punishment, although a slap when you are annoyed will not cause resentment and can even be beneficial. It is the cold-blooded, rule-book, self-righteous type of physical punishment that builds up future trouble. Nagging—by which I mean constant verbal reminders to behave, or rubbing in the results of bad behaviour— will be equally ineffective. It is easier for your child to turn a deaf ear than to mend his behaviour. He may do this quite literally, so that you begin to suspect he is deaf. Do not appeal to his good nature or to his love for you. ("Poor mummy! You make mummy so sad.") If you do, you are dealing in an expendable commodity. It will be easier for him to become callous and say "your feelings be damned". Above all, don't claim that it makes you ill or that if he goes on being a bad boy he will hasten your end. Emotionally—if he has another parent to fall back on—it may pay him just to write you off. If there is no other parent upon whom he can rely, such tactics are likely to induce in him destructive conflicts and guilt feelings. He cannot afford to become independent of you, yet resents your taking an unfair advantage of his attachment. Above all, do not threaten to have him sent away to a school or otherwise "put away". This can only produce insecurity and have other dire consequences.

In positive terms, the conditioning process should ensure that it pays the child to learn to control himself. The rewards of doing so and the disadvantages of not doing so should both be immediate. In our Centre we recommend the following behaviour modification programme for parents to use at home. It is based on a weekly allowance which is entirely dependent upon the child's good behaviour. You decide what a reasonable weekly allowance should be, and divide it into seven parts. (There should be no incidental sources of finance, such as money for the movies or bus fares for a treat.) He earns one of the seven parts each day, but only receives it when he has gone to bed at night (because going to bed itself may be a source of friction). If he has a lapse at any time during the day, you simply say, (assuming a daily allowance of five cents) "That's one cent gone", or "You've saved me a cent by doing that". Your tone should be dispassionate, and you may even feign a mild triumph because he has saved you a little money. Unlike the explosive reaction, this punishment does not afford him the gratification of producing an emotional effect on you. The only visible result of his bad behaviour is that you have scored a point, and he has lost out correspondingly. If his misdemeanour is more than usually serious you can deduct two cents, and let this be seen as a mark of your grave displeasure. But never dock the whole five cents at once—that would be squandering your ammunition and you would be at his mercy for the rest of the day. This form of behaviour modification has worked very well with boys of six to seven years of age. One mother who used it came back to me after two weeks in a state of great anxiety: her boy had become so good that she feared there must be something wrong with him!

Children who are a little older but not yet adolescent may defeat the plan by becoming unconcerned about money. Then you will have to consider a point system upon which treats or some coveted toy depend. Make the rewards positive gratifications rather than deprivations, that is to say, something a little extra rather than something forfeited. Do not reject such a scheme because it looks like bribery. After all, the world "bribes" by rewarding those whose behaviour is effective and acceptable. The anxiety about bribery arises from the expectation that children should be actuated by high moral motives. Few adults are.

Behaviour modification is not, of course, the whole, or even the main answer. Those who believe in it uncritically maintain that undesirable behaviour will get less or disappear merely by ignoring it. Their fallacy is to assume that the seeking of attention is the sole motive for misbehaviour. Therefore, they argue, if you ignore it the child desists because he does not find it rewarding. Any parent of an inconsequent child knows better than that. If he cannot get any response from you by one type of attention-seeking behaviour he may well give it up only to try an even more extreme type. The last state will then be worse than the first. Moreover, the inconsequent child gets much positive fun out of showing off, noisiness, thoughtless experimentation, meddling and producing emotional reactions in adults. More and more he indulges in them as compensations for his academic failure.

Over the years the inconsequent child slowly learns, by painful experience, to control his behaviour in the standard situations of everyday life. He learns not to annoy people, and how to do everyday jobs sensibly without hurting himself or breaking things. Particularly, when he reaches adolescence, his heightened need for companionship with boys and girls of his own age makes him control his impulses in order to be socially acceptable. Throughout life he learns how to seal off the dangerous areas; but a new situation may catch him unawares.

If his earlier bad relationships with his age-mates have left him insecure about acceptance, he may become an easily led young man and yield to suggestions from mischievous associates. At a stag party some one may remark what fun it would be to hold a lighted match under the heat-sensitive fire sprinkler. Up he jumps and does just that, with consequences that could have been foreseen if he had given himself a split second to foresee them. Such youths are easily led into delinquent escapades either out of a sheer desire for comradeship or because they cannot bear the taunt of "chickening out".

The training of the inconsequent child consists, therefore, in patiently conditioning him to use foresight in situation after situation, and not getting unduly discouraged at his lapses. When a lapse occurs, divert your own anger by analysing it. What was there in the situation for which he was unprepared? Were his resources of control impaired because he was

In playing learning games young impulsive children are often too impatient to wait their turn. The Merry-Go-Rounds puzzle trains them to overcome this difficulty. Each player has alternate pieces of the circle, so that neither can make any progress unless he waits for the other to place his piece.

Photo courtesy of Guelph Mercury

tired, hungry or ill? Had your conditioning schedule—
that is to say, your responses to his behaviour—become inconsistent lately? Is some other member of
the family failing to support you by encouraging
or giving in to his bad behaviour, or opposing your
efforts in his hearing? The more you are able to
think back and analyse the less you will feel threatened and discouraged. .

Of course you will have many lapses yourself.
Don't take these too seriously. You have to go
through a process of conditioning yourself, and the
remorse you feel is a necessary part of it. Moreover,
the hasty action or the unjust punishment will not
have the disastrous effects you anticipate. Children
make allowances for the bad temper and irritability
of adults, and learn from them. If you succeeded in
bringing up your child without this sort of experience
you would be coddling him in an unreal world.

However, reacting to inconsequent behaviour by
harshness is likely to lead to disagreements between
the parents, even to the extent of endangering their
marriage. But the effects of avoidance are more insidi-
ous. Either or both of the parents expose themselves
to a chronic source of stress in the form of an undisci-
plined child who rules their lives. It needs only some
other setback, such as an accident, illness, job anxieties, disagreeable work conditions or financial worries
for the cumulative stresses to exceed the limits of
tolerance. Finding the child a source of discord
between herself and her husband, the mother may
panic and turn on the child, joining her husband in
threats to have him "put away". The state of stress
behaviour, described in the next chapter, ensues, and

the child, being the most exposed object, bears the brunt of the attack. Whatever you do as parents, work out and practise a common strategy.

6

The Hostile child

Turning
inconsequence
into hostility One of the most telltale indica-
tions of the reasons for over-
reacting behaviour is the balance
between inconsequence and hos-
tility. We obtain scores for each of these basic types
of maladjustment by asking the child's teacher to
complete an assessment form[1] which offers an objective means of describing how the child behaves in
school. If the child has a high score for inconsequence,
but little or none for hostility, we are sure that his
parents have been able to cope with his impulsive
behaviour without rejecting him. If there is a high
hostility score without much inconsequence, we know
that we are dealing with a temperamentally vulnerable child who feels rejected by his parents. If we
find that the scores for inconsequence and hostility

1. D.H. Stott and N.C. Marston, *The Bristol Social Adjustment
   Guides and Manual*, 1971 revision. Toronto, Musson Book
   Co.; San Diego, Educational and Industrial Testing Service;
   London, University of London Press.

are both high it is a fairly safe bet that we have another case of the vicious circle of stress, rejection and hostility on our hands. The child's inconsequent behaviour has become more than the parents can put up with. In their anger they give way to threats which undermine his faith in their loyalty to him. He shows his resentment by committing acts calculated to annoy them still more. They make more threats, and possibly try to carry them out. His hostility takes on a more determined form, and he vents it on other adults, including his teachers.

This unhappy state of affairs can so easily arise when there is an inconsequent child in the family that it must be considered in detail. The failure of the child to respond to normal disciplinary measures reduces the parents to a state of helplessness. The father may feel it as a challenge to his authority and effectiveness as a parent, the mother as a measure of her failure to give affection. Deciding that the boy is a "bad lot" the father becomes punitive and threatens to take him to court as unmanageable. The mother sticks up for the child, and he becomes a focus of quarrelling between the parents. So long as a child has one parent he can rely on, he can endure the antagonism of the other. When both turn against him his position becomes intolerable.

Hostility as an affection-killing reaction
A child who becomes convinced that his parents don't want him is emotionally in the same position as that of the jilted lover. In order to destroy his love for parents whom he sees as being faithless to him he replaces it by hatred. He

looks for ways of punishing them for their disloyalty
and of making the breach as wide as possible. His
manner becomes sullen, he stays away from home
and deliberately chooses to do things, like stealing
from members of the household or neighbours, which
are calculated to make his parents angry. He will
seek rejection, because to know the worst is more
bearable than intolerable anxiety. Sometimes a boy
who wonders whether his father will stick by him
commits a further delinquent act just to test him.
Hostility in a child is, in sum, a reaction to the fear of
being deserted. Until this is recognized there is a
danger that well-meaning parents will go on making
things worse by threats, such as that he will be sent
to a school for naughty boys, which they think will
scare him into mending his ways. Once, on the other
hand, such threats cease, and the boy becomes convinced that his parents are determined to keep him in
the family, the hostility—since it is no longer needed
as an affection-killing reaction—may disappear with
dramatic suddenness.

Threats of the mother to desert the home, even
though uttered in times of exasperation without her
really intending to do so, may have the same effect
of undermining her child's confidence in her. Not
being able to stand the uncertainty of wondering
whether she will still be there on his return from
school, he sets out to cut himself off from her
emotionally, and to do this he has to suppress his
love with hostility. It seems contradictory that a boy
should commit hostile acts against the parent towards
whom he is most attached—until we recall the analogy
of the jilted lover. The hostility may alternate with

phases of over-attention. In his anxiety over his mother the boy makes strenuous efforts—by way of helping in the home, buying her expensive presents and wanting to give her nearly all his earnings—to dissuade her, as he thinks, from running away. The moral of all this is that it is not wise to utter threats to clear out, even light-heartedly or in irritation. It may not affect some children at all, but others will take it to heart.

The danger point comes in the life of a family when one of the parents is subjected to other severe stresses. One of the reasons for the rise in the delinquency rate in Europe after the Second World War was the inability of fathers who had been torpedoed or were the victims of shock from explosion to tolerate the enterprising mischief of an inconsequent child. Accidents and illness can have the same effect of reducing resistance to stress. This may happen to a mother if she becomes depressed and exhausted as a result of marital quarrels, or as an outcome of grief on losing her husband. Every experienced probation officer has had a mother bringing her son to him with the demand, "Take him off my hands, if he remains in my house any longer I shall murder him"— or words to that effect. A mother in this state of vicious rejection and intolerance is probably at heart exceedingly fond of her son and has always taken good care of him. Two weeks later, when the Probation Officer has arranged for the boy to be brought to the Juvenile Court as unmanageable, the mother may have recovered her better feelings and strongly resist the idea that he be taken from her. But the damage may have been done. The harsh words were uttered in the boy's hearing, and he has lost confidence in his mother's loyalty.

A child's resentfulness against the destruction of his sense of security may remain at simmering point until, in turn, his nervous reserves are shattered by some accident or illness, or by the blow of losing contact with a relative or neighbour who has offered him solace and refuge. Then, quite suddenly, he may run away from home or break out in a round of desperate delinquency. In such a mood he loses interest in his own future. To show his parents up, as he thinks, he makes up his mind to go bad.

Tensions centring around the learning-disabled child

These are admittedly crisis situations, but to a lesser degree they can be found in many ordinary families. Often they centre around a child's learning disability. In this age when formal paper qualifications are the tickets of entry to nearly all white-collar jobs, bad school reports, the child's apparent lack of concern and will to work, and the knowledge that in what interests him he is not stupid, are apt to make the parents frantic with frustration. It does not help if the Principal simply regards the child as a non-academic type who should follow a vocational programme. Perhaps he will be most happy and effective in a so-called manual job. But even now many trades require fluent reading ability and understanding of blueprints. The number of jobs depending mainly on muscles is small and diminishes every year. Hence it is no longer a matter of parents being over-ambitious for their children. Their anxiety has a real foundation.

Parental frustration generates the primitive reactions of attack or avoidance. The attack can take the form of sarcastic remarks, unfavourable comparisons with brothers and sisters and the high-achieving children of friends, and a general attitude of soured disappointment. The child becomes the educational "black sheep of the family". With time, the frustration generates avoidance: the father or mother or both lose interest and reject the boy.

Hostility as a learning handicap
Both the hostility and the anxiety that alternates with it become emotional blocks to learning. One good way of expressing hostility to a parent is to do poorly at school. I once knew a formerly delinquent but academically very able boy who would periodically go into sullen, hostile moods, and at these times he would do badly at every task, whether it be in the workshop or schoolroom. It was quite obvious that his motive was a determination not to please or earn approval.

I remember also a little girl of eight in a school for the trainable retarded whose fashionable and socially ambitious mother was obviously ashamed of her. The girl showed by her many bright remarks that she was not really mentally handicapped, but she cultivated the pose in order to get even with her mother. She played the role with convincing skill, but like the numerous "dull" and "retarded" who do the same she gave herself away. We were teaching her the sound values of the letters by playing the Holder Game with the Touch Cards.[2] She had to show which of the four cards had the correct picture on the reverse side, as indicated by the letters on the sides she could see. Thus, by pure chance, she should have had one in four right. We wondered why she never seemed to get any right at all. One day she did get one right, but quickly "corrected" it to make it wrong.

I came across another instance of false retardation produced by hostility when, several years later, on a visit to a school for the trainable retarded, I was greeted by a well-built youth with words that ran like this, "It is with great pleasure, Dr. Stott, that we students welcome you to our school. We hope you will enjoy your visit, etc., etc.". On my leaving I was treated to a similar speech. Few mayors or politicians could have done better. Yet, this youth was completely illiterate. He had a soured attitude to people, and a bad reputation in the neighbourhood. When he left the school he used to hang around the town and make a nuisance of himself by going into stores, purchasing articles and then a few minutes later returning them and demanding his money back. His evidently normal mental ability had been stunted by an anti-social motivation.

These are admittedly striking and exceptional cases where a cultivated strategy of hostility produces a retardation which is none the less real. For every one of them there are a hundred in which the student has no interest in doing well at school because he no

2. Item I of the Programmed Reading Kit—see Appendix A.

longer wishes to afford satisfaction to his parents. This attitude extends itself to his teachers. He comes to prefer the role of outcast as far as adults are concerned. This leads him to repudiate their standards of conduct, and to choose as associates those who feel the same way. Needless to say, they throw away their educational opportunities. Most of them simply drop out of school. A few re-surface as delinquents.

There is a twofold remedy to the vicious circle of disappointment and rejection. First, don't make the child's failure a family issue. Once normal encouragement, interest and reminders are seen to have no effect, don't think that angry nagging or browbeating will do any more good. The second aspect of the remedy rests upon the truism that action chases away anxiety. So get busy with a home-learning programme. If you are not confident that you have the patience to carry it out yourself, if the vicious circle of frustration and mutual rejection has gone too far, or you are counselled not to attempt it yourself, obtain some tutoring help.

Finding a tutor It is, however, not good enough simply to employ a tutor and leave it at that. Private tutoring, even when given by a qualified teacher, often doesn't work out. The tension of having to produce answers for even half an hour upon a subject with which one is having difficulties is more than a human being can stand. I can quote from my own experience as a pupil. When I was preparing for a college entrance examination I was tutored in Latin by a teacher who kept me struggling at a text for a solid hour at a time. On one occasion, when I had probably seemed to him—as a learned classical scholar—even more than usually slow, he kept me for an hour and a half. Then I had a sudden vision of his bony figure wading ashore from a Roman galley complete with helmet and shield and his pants rolled up to his knees. I began to roar with laughter. Each time he asked me what I was laughing at, the thought of telling him made me laugh the louder. In the end he gave up and threw me out of his house. Without intending to, I had sought relief from the tension by an hysterical avoidance mechanism. Under similar pressures the children who have to struggle ineffectively through reading texts will utilize a wide variety of avoidance mechanisms—bursting into tears, making remarks about quite different subjects showing that their minds are not on the task at all, or developing physical symptoms such as sickness or aches and pains.

Whatever type of tutor you employ, see that the sessions are rendered enjoyable by a game method. If a qualified teacher is not available try to find a college or high-school student who will be glad of the money and the experience. Such a tutor may show better understanding and be more easily accepted by your child because of the smaller age-gap.

The Unforthcoming child

Origins of unforthcomingness

Like inconsequence, unforthcomingness is a handicap of temperament. I use this word with Stella Chess[1] to mean the basic behaviour style of an individual which sets the stamp on all his dealings with the world.

We have failed to recognize unforthcomingness as a handicap of temperament because, test-minded, we were satisfied with "low intelligence", as an explanation of the unforthcoming child's failure to respond. Even though a tester would often see that a child was not doing his best owing to lack of confidence, it was not realized to what extent such a general fear of the unknown would, over the years, limit the child's experience and powers of thought so that he could become mentally retarded in the literal sense of the term.

1. Stella Chess, "Temperament and learning ability of school children," *American Journal of Public Health*, Dec. 1968.

I would estimate that the vast majority of children who score IQ's between 50 and 85, and quite a few of the under 50's, are in this so-called intelligence range chiefly because of this temperamental handicap. Several years ago, when I was making a study of a series of slow-learning children in order to try to get at the reasons for their handicaps, I found that I never seemed to find a child who was "just dull". In every case that I examined there was a mixture of temperamental handicaps, emotional stresses arising from severe family anxieties, social disadvantages, erratic schooling, long-standing ill-health, any of which would have been sufficient to account for the academic failure. Surely, I thought, there must be some dull children. So I asked the teachers of four schools for the educable retarded (covering the IQ range from 50 to 85) to go carefully through their class registers and pick out for me those whom they regarded as simply of low intelligence, without behavioural, emotional, social or health handicaps. They willingly agreed, thinking they had plenty of them. When I asked for the lists they told me rather apologetically that they could find fewer than they thought. In all, eighteen were nominated. Of these I made a careful study, getting detailed assessments of their behaviour in school and interviewing their parents to obtain a picture of their home background and their development from birth. In not one case did I have to conclude that the child must have been genetically dull. There were some who were multiple-impaired. Because of their health and behavioural handicaps it was impossible to find out to what extent they were also mentally impaired. With our latest techniques designed to overcome handicaps of learning behaviour I think we could have gone some way in doing so, but I did not then have these aids at my disposal. I could not therefore assert dogmatically that none of them were born dull. But I did not have to fall back on the idea that there were any who were dull because they received a poor deal in the sharing out of "intelligence".

In other words, the nice curves of intelligence that the psychometrists produce, with the people of average intelligence in the middle bulge, and a tail of the bright at one end and of the dull at the other, hide a mass of fallacies. But how can it be possible, once again I hear the incredulous reader murmur, that so many highly intelligent experts, who can do complicated statistics quite beyond the capability of the average man or woman, could be so mistaken? The answer is precisely that they have only looked at figures, they have never looked at children—or if they have they have seen them only as containers of something called intelligence. They are ignorant of the behavioural, emotional, social, educational and health handicaps which drag children down to the lower end of that famous curve. What would we think of a microbiologist who never looked down a microscope, or an astronomer who never looked through a telescope? Surely honest observation is the ABC of any science.

Since unforthcomingness has not generally been recognized for what it is, we must not be surprised to find that little research has been done on its causes. It has been found to be associated with stresses and ill health of the mother during the pregnancy[2]. Among rats a similar state has been observed in those of the young whose mothers were subjected to fear of electric shock during the pregnancy (without however having the shock administered after conception). As with inconsequence, unforthcomingness can in nearly all cases be traced back to very early life, and within a single family one child may have the handicap and the others not. Joy Adamson[3] describes the unventuresomeness and timidity of one of the cubs of the lioness that she reared. This cub was a typical unforthcoming child. Yet it would be ridiculous to claim that within a few days the mother lioness had treated it differently from the other two. Mrs. Adamson points out that there is usually one such timid animal in every litter of lion cubs, and this one survives only when food is so plentiful that there is enough to go round without its having to fight to get its share. In sum, the probability is that unforthcomingness is congenital, that is to say, that it dates from birth or before. It is not in any sense due to the way in which the child has been brought up.

Vulnerability of temperament　　When I speak of a condition such as a handicap of temperament being congenital, social workers and other kindly people are inclined to rear up in

2. D.H. Stott, "Evidence for prenatal impairment of temperament in mentally retarded children," *Vita Humana*, Vol. 8, 1971.
3. Joy Adamson, *Living Free*, Collins, 1961.

indignation. They feel that it condemns a child always to have the handicap, and nullifies their own efforts. The opposite is mostly true. Some congenital handicaps are irremediable, but many take the form of predispositions or weaknesses. If a child has a liability to respiratory troubles—which is likely to be inborn and indeed genetic—the doctor will advise extra care against infections. He may also point out, quite rightly, that the child will probably grow out of the weakness. In the same manner, temperamental handicaps take the form of vulnerabilities. The inconsequent child is vulnerable to those situations in which he is tempted to show off or to attempt foolhardy feats. The unforthcoming child is vulnerable in the face of strangeness or difficulty. Children of both types can be helped to overcome their weaknesses.

Getting over unforth-comingness Stella Chess describes the sort of child whom I have named unforthcoming as "slow to warm up". This is an accurate description of the mildly affected child, and it is a valuable one because it stresses that she can in fact "warm up", and does not suffer from an irremediable handicap. Her apprehensiveness may be viewed as an extreme form of caution and dislike of failure. Every individual weighs up a problem in terms of his ability to solve it. If he decides he is strong, clever or knowledgeable enough to do so, he tackles it. If he feels himself too weak or not clever or knowledgeable enough he evades it. This process of appraisal in terms of "I can" or "I can't" is essential to our well-being. If a person overestimates his powers, he runs into failure or disas-

71

ter. If he underestimates his abilities he does not use them and achieves little. This latter is the weakness of the unforthcoming child.

The remedy lies in training her, in ways that have been described in Chapter II, to develop an attitude of "I can do it". By these means she gradually learns to make a more confident estimate of her abilities. We must not, however, be disappointed if her apprehensiveness and freezing reappear in an unaccustomed situation. What we really do by any conditioning process is to train the person (or animal) to respond in a certain way in particular types of situations. The effects of the training will extend to other situations only in so far as the child sees in them certain familiar features which encourage her to feel that she can cope with them also. Thus the training of the unforthcoming child in confidence is a long-term job which demands great care. If, after having partly learned to read, she is thrown into a classroom situation where an unfamiliar method is being used or she feels pressured or harassed, she will once again withdraw behind the pose of dullness.

Please, therefore, if you are the parent of an unforthcoming girl or boy, don't go to the Principal of the school, wave this book in his face and—pointing out that Dr. Stott says your child is not dull—demand that she or he be taken out of a special class. This is one type of child who needs the security of a protected learning environment, without frequent changes of teachers or the need to make friends among new sets of classmates. A severely unforthcoming child needs to remain in a special class for at least two years. In an impersonal and insensitive atmosphere she will retreat into dullness. Naturally, special training, or self-training, as well as exceptional concern and insight, are needed in these teachers of special classes, and your child will be happier and make better progress with such a one than in the regular classroom.

Growing out of unforth- comingness Luckily, some unforthcoming children grow out of their handicap. I suspect that this happens more often with boys than girls, as in the case of asthma and some other health conditions found more often in boys; but this may be because I have had better opportunities to study boys than girls over a long term. It is not uncommon to find adolescent boys in a vocational school for the "non-academic" who are poor readers but surprisingly able at some vocational skill. They are also businesslike and healthily assertive. Yet in their records we read repeatedly such phrases as "lacks confidence", "needs to come out of his shell", "afraid to try". Their tragedy is that, during their pre-adolescent unforthcomingness, no one recognized their handicap, so that they were treated as dull children. It was accepted that they would learn little because they were regarded as being incapable of learning more. During puberty something has happened to restore their motivation, and they have become emotionally normal young men—but with an educational lag of many years.

I had one such boy in the club for the educationally backward described in Chapter 10. He had made himself so proficient at card tricks that I could not see how he did them. Learning to do card tricks—with the risk of failure and ridicule before a group—needs, I reflected, quite a lot of confidence. Consulting his school records and enquiring of his teachers, I learned that until puberty he had been so timid that it was hopeless (with the techniques used at the time) to teach him to read.

Thus, while never pressing an unforthcoming child, we should not allow her or him to fall into the position of being a non-learner. For every such child a careful individual progress plan should be drawn up. It will probably have to be modified from time to time, upwards or downwards, as the temperamental handicap and the hitherto concealed mental ability are more accurately assessed. But there should always be a goal to work towards, however modest it may be. It need not necessarily be one of academic achievement, because the child may first have to learn to cope with play activities. Once he or she has gained a little confidence in these, she can go on to games which teach number and reading.

Dependence   Sometimes an unforthcoming little girl—or so she appears to be—makes an outstanding recovery, to the extent that she becomes a good mixer, demands new tasks and even becomes temporarily badly behaved and disruptive. When one looks back at her shy, helpless earlier state one realizes that there was too much strategy in it. I have been able to work with two little girls of this type in a nursery for the retarded. One of them was considered extremely retarded by all who had dealings with her. She would not play with toys or

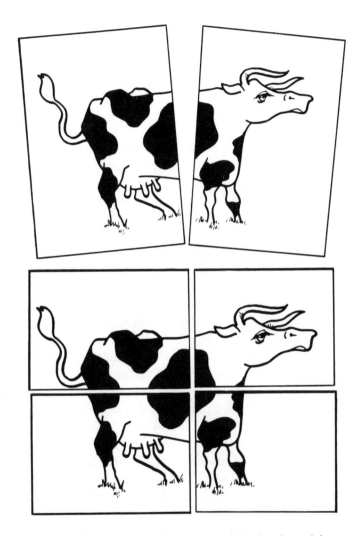

The Flying Start Learning-to-Learn Kit *begins with activities which do not frighten the most timid and are within the attention span of the most distractible.*

with other children, nor join in the singing circle. Her standard pattern of behaviour was to lie on the floor and mope. The volunteer staff of the nursery took pity on her, and picked her up and cuddled her, so that she was nearly always to be seen, a picture of misery, huddled in someone's arms. Only her active eyes betrayed her: she was observing the effects of her actions on other people. Her mother said that at home she would have a temper tantrum when she couldn't get what she wanted. Following a behaviour-modification programme, we allowed her to lie on the floor until she got bored and saw that she was no longer securing the attentions of the too-affectionate helpers. Progressively she began to play with toys and with other children, in between desperate efforts to revert to her previous dependency. In our Centre she became an active child and enjoyed playing the phonic games, at which she showed more than average ability for her age. She even scored an IQ in the normal range! The truth was that fundamentally she was anything but the typical unforthcoming child, who is content to play a very unassuming and un-ambitious role. She had evolved a very effective strategy for controlling her world. It was not that she did this wilfully as a completely stable child. She had had an abnormal birth and her development had been delayed. Not until she was eighteen months old did she smile at people or show any other signs of wanting affection. When the need for it was awak-ened in her, she demanded all she could get, even if it meant having to remain a baby.

The second four-year-old had developed a pattern of dependency which, while it lasted, was indistinguishable from unforthcomingness. She was reluctant to try anything new and would not speak to strangers, blocking her mouth with her thumb and hiding her face behind her hands. After a few months, in a summer programme run by some of my psychology students, she decided to copy the ways of a very active and amusing little boy who got a lot of attention owing to his charm of manner. Quite suddenly, from being shy and withdrawn, she became hyperactive and disruptive. She had decided to experiment with a new strategy that might get her more attention. After a few weeks she adjusted herself and entered Kindergarten as an active, happy child.

Both these little girls would almost certainly have maintained their strategy of helpless, apparently retarded dependency without the benefit of a behaviour modification and learning-to-learn programme in which all the adults in their lives co-operated. They afford us further instances of the impossibility of discovering a child's capacity so long as his mode of behaviour keeps him from using it.

8

Perceptual handicap and dyslexia

*What about
perceptual
handicap?*
The inconsequent children that
I have described in Chapter 5
are often diagnosed as "perceptually handicapped". This is one
convenient way of explaining why it is that, although
they seem to have the intelligence, they cannot learn
in school. To appreciate the shallowness of such a
diagnosis we need only have another look at a few
of these children and see how they are using their
perceptual powers. Immediately it becomes apparent
that they are no more using them properly than they
are using their brains in general properly. They do not
give themselves time to get the information, whether
it be about a shape or a word. Their handicap is a behavioural one, namely that of not paying attention.
Their hyperactivity and impulsiveness do not give
their perceptual abilities a chance. If anyone is inclined to doubt this let him try to find a perceptually
handicapped child with a stable, cautious temperament who takes the time needed to work out a prob-

This simplest form of the Merry-Go-Round puzzle aims to teach the impulsive child just one thing: to cooperate with another child in taking turns in a game. The circle-shape has a fascination for many hyperactive children whom it is difficult to interest in anything else.

lem. His task will be like that of the Greek philosopher Diogenes who set out to find an honest man!

The best way of convincing a doubter that a so-called perceptual handicap is really a behavioural handicap is to have him observe a child of this sort playing the Mail Box game of our Flying Start Learning-to-Learn Kit. At first he mails the letters hastily without taking the time to notice the difference between, say, an *h* and an *n*, a *u* and an *n*, a *b* and a *d*. But once the partner-child checks them by matching up the half-pictures on the backs of the letter cards and calls out "Wrong", he realizes that he will have to proceed more carefully. He moves the card carefully from box to box to make certain that the letters correspond. In other words, he learns to attend and to bring his perceptual powers into play. Then he makes correct choices, and demonstrates that there is nothing wrong with his perception. If, however, he were given a test of perceptual ability before being trained to attend and to reflect, he would certainly be rated as perceptually handicapped.

I can honestly say that, among the hundreds of children with learning disabilities with whom I have worked, I have never had to label one as perceptually handicapped apart from those whose severe brain damage has impaired their mental functioning as a whole. No doubt individual differences will appear in any test of perceptual ability which stretches people's powers of discrimination to the limit. It is unlikely that we are all the same perceptually any more than we are alike in any other function. But the lower limit would be well above what is needed for efficient reading. Notably, one does not find children, apart from the rare cases of severe brain damage that I have mentioned, who cannot distinguish between the letters of the alphabet once they have been trained to attend to them.

I have even had children referred to me by a well-known neurologist as perceptually handicapped, only to find once again that the problem lay in their behaviour. One of these children, a boy of about nine years, amused himself while waiting for me by making a drawing of the ships and cranes that he could view on the river from my office window. It showed excellent powers of observation and was accurate in a way which ruled out any possibility of his being perceptually handicapped. Another was a girl of thirteen who was able at a glance to read words on a paper lying a few feet away at a diagonally upsidedown angle. Her trouble was that she was flighty and hyperactive, and I suspected that she was also trading on her supposed disability.

Errors of sequence   There are indeed some children who suffer from a neurological disability which upsets the order in which they do things. When they speak their words often get jumbled up with one another, as if—as their mothers describe it—they are trying to get them all out at once. Similarly, their limbs get out of sequence, so that they trip up, knock things over, or are otherwise clumsy. If they are also impetuous in their actions the reader will recognize in this description the inconsequent child. Not all such children speak in a jumbled way, or are motor-impaired, but the risk of their having these speech or motor handicaps is several times greater than in a behaviourally well-adjusted child.

Reversal Reading from right to left, and
errors confusing *b* and *d*, are often
regarded as evidence of a percep-
tual handicap. We have to view these confusions of
direction in their proper perspective. One of the first
things a baby has to learn is that he is looking at the
same objects whichever way round they are. Mother
and father are the same people whether they are
facing to the right or to the left. A chair is a chair
however it is placed. If a child did not make this
valuable generalization he could never make sense of
his world. Only when he comes to deal with letters
and numbers does he have to unlearn all this. Now the
interesting thing is that, as Pavlov showed, unlearning
is, strictly speaking, impossible. What really happens
is not that the original learning is erased, but that it
has to be continually corrected by another piece of
learning. The original learning remains embedded in
the brain, and in time may re-emerge if it is more
strongly implanted than the correction. Consequently,
in remembering to read or write from the left, or
that *b* faces one way and *d* the other, a child has to
build very firm directional corrections into his learning. Once he has done so, he has to allow his brain
time for two processes to take place. On both these
counts the inconsequent child is at a disadvantage.
He does not give himself enough time to note and
reflect about direction, so that the new learning which
says, "This is one of those special cases where it *does*
matter from which end I begin, or which way it

In putting together the What's Happening puzzles the child has to look at a picture to see a logical connection. This trains him to think about what he sees.

faces", has not time to get properly established. And, acting over-rapidly as he does, he may not allow time for the second of the processes, the new learning about direction, to cancel out the old learning. Once again, we see that a behavioural handicap lies at the root of the learning disability.

This is a far cry from the claims that these children actually see the world in some queer, distorted way. If, to them, everything is upsidedown or reversed they would have no perceptual difficulty. Psychologists who have experimented with glasses which turn things upsidedown, or reverse right and left, have found that after a short time the wearers' brains carried out the corrections: they saw things the right way up and the right way round. The notion that the so-called perceptually handicapped child sees the world differently is derived no doubt from his clumsiness. He may bang into, trip over, knock down, spill things. But this can be explained in part by a general characteristic of his behaviour, namely his impetuousness, and in part by his genuine motor impairment, that is to say, his inability to control and coordinate his limbs.

Why the myth? In sum, the notion that any significant number of children are perceptually handicapped is a myth. If this is true, you as a reader have a right to ask why, in these supposedly enlightened times, when students of psychology spend years in getting Ph.Ds and millions of dollars are spent annually on research, a myth of such proportions could have gained currency and persist. The first reason is that

The ordinary type of jig-saw, with its varied shapes, tempts the impulsive child to try one piece after another at random. He cannot do this with the Animal Puzzles because all the pieces are similar. He has to take the time to look at the picture.

The first set (above) are cut into six pieces, the second (below) into ten.

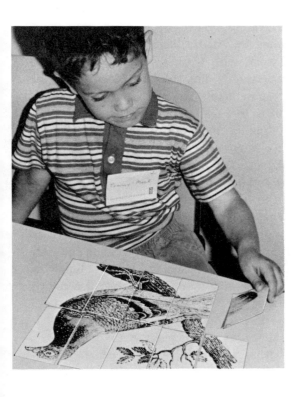

nearly all research in this field consists in testing groups of children. The tester is not usually the professor who has the research grant but a research assistant, and he—or usually she—does what she is told without, as a junior member of the team, having the confidence to question the whole theoretical basis of the study. The existence of a perceptual handicap is apparently confirmed because the inattentive, hyperactive inconsequent children get low scores on any test of perceptual ability. The professor does not realize what is happening because he sees little of the children, and in any case he is chiefly interested in getting results to write up in an article or to report at a conference. From a career point of view he is doing the right thing. If he spent five years in personal work with learning-disabled children in order to understand why they failed to learn, he might find that he hadn't any neatly designed experiment to report. In an academic environment where the rule is "publish or perish" he would not get promotion, and might even find himself out of a job.

The second reason for the growth and persistence of the myth of perceptual handicap has been the comfort that it has brought to parents. To have a child of nine or more years old who cannot read must be a source of constant frustration and anxiety to educated people who appreciate what a disaster illiteracy can be in a literate society. It is less humiliating if his failure to learn can be explained away as some mysterious but scientifically plausible defect in perception. The parents are at least reassured that they do not have mental deficiency in the family.

I hope that, if you are the parent of a learning-disabled child such as I have described, you will bear in mind what I have said about intelligence, and no longer feel that you have to defend yourself against the suspicion of mental deficiency by seizing upon the idea of perceptual handicap.

Dyslexia   Dyslexia is another term which has acquired a high sounding respectability. It is taken from the Greek, and means nothing more than "bad at reading". So any child who is bad at reading can be called a dyslexic. But where does that get us? A friend of mine once went to the doctor and was told that he had "rhinitis". When he looked up the word in a dictionary he found it was connected with the Greek "rhino"—that which is to do with the nose. The doctor could have told him he had a cold in the nose.

Dyslexia has come to mean something more than being bad at reading. The term is used to imply that the child suffers from some mysterious condition, an older term for which was "word-blindness". Literally, it is preposterous that a person could be blind to words and yet be able to see other objects, except as an extreme form of avoidance, or refusal to see. (This, however, was not what was meant by those who used the term.) No rational explanation has been given of such an extraordinary phenomenon. The word dyslexia is, in effect, an explanation-by-label when no other reason for the disability can be found. We can deceive ourselves that we have explained something just by giving it a name. In this way we avoid the frustration of having to admit our ignorance, and it saves us the trouble of searching for a better understanding.

Myths can be dangerous

To diagnose a reading disability as the result of a perceptual handicap, or to see it as a mysterious dyslexia may be a serious disadvantage to the child because he may get the wrong treatment, or no treatment at all. If the source of his trouble is believed to be that he sees the world in a distorted way in relation to his own body, months or years may be wasted in having him crawl about on all fours and perform similarly useless exercises, when he should be learning how to sit on a chair and develop his powers of attention. If he is believed to be a dyslexic no attempt may be made to teach him to read, or to train him in good learning habits. And the child is often bright enough to pick up and exploit a diagnosis of perceptual handicap or dyslexia as an excuse for his avoidance of reading. It also acts as a kind of compensation for his self-esteem: he is somebody special and unique who will not be expected to face up to the responsibilities of growing up. Being taken for testing from clinic to clinic may well have an effect like this on a child, especially if—as often happens—the supposed disability is discussed in his presence.

9

How children learn to read

Over the past two generations expert opinion about how to teach reading has swung this way and that. The time-honoured method was to drill the child in the sounds which the letters represented so that, presumably, he could build up words by blending the sounds together. This, the traditional phonic method, seems an obvious, straightforward way of teaching children to read. However, it did not succeed with some, and this caused the method as a whole to be called in question. The reading experts of the time seized upon a psychological theory which was coming into prominence at that time. The central idea in it was that the way a shape is perceived depends upon its background.

Basically the theory was a useful one, but it was wrongly applied to the process of learning to read. The college reading specialists argued that words had to be seen as wholes, and insisted that phonic teaching should be banned. For a whole generation teachers were bullied into teaching reading by sight methods. Children were expected to be able to recognize words by their shapes. As any person of common sense could have guessed, the results were disastrous. They would have been still more so if children had not worked out the phonic code for themselves or been taught it by their parents. But such was the complacency and so great was the subservience to the supposed experts that it needed the shock of the Russian Sputnik and the exposure of Rudolph Flesch's *Why Johnny Can't Read*[1] to expose the failures of the sight method.

The result was a wholesale reversion to phonics. The trouble now was that none of the college reading specialists had any experience of teaching by the phonic method. Neither they nor the large publishers who rushed out series of phonic readers realized that the phonic method is almost as susceptible to error as is teaching by sight methods. The result is that we are in danger of repeating the mistakes of our grandparents. A certain number of children will not get the phonic idea because of a general ignorance about how the child's mind grasps and utilizes the phonic code.

This puts you, as a parent, in a tricky position. The teacher of your child can be at any of the above stages in her thinking and practice. She may be using a mixture of methods, or she may have decided to develop an approach of her own that she finds effective with most children.

The sight method   It would be comforting if we could regard the sight method as dead and buried. However, many teachers, especially those of Grade One and of

1. Rudolf Flesch, *Why Johnny Can't Read*, Harper Bros, New York, 1955.

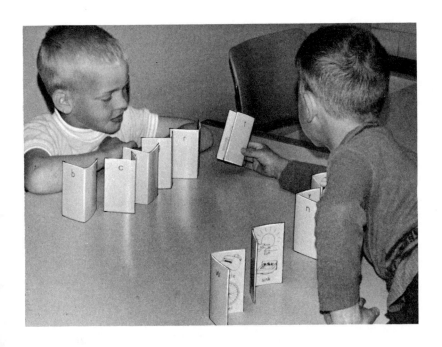

The First-letter Cards are stood
up so that each player can see
the pictures on his cards, but the
letters only on the other player's
cards. There are four pictures on
each card, and a player can name
any one of them. In this way
they learn to hear the same
sound at the beginnings of different words.

special classes, still hold to the view that children should learn to read a number of words, or even sentences, by sight recognition before being let into the secret of the phonic code. In schools for the retarded it is still common practice to try to teach the students a certain number of "experience words" such as *Ladies, Men, Crosswalk* by sight methods. It may be that you as a parent have been advised to practise a number of sight words, written boldly on cards, with your learning-disabled child. Or you may have bought a programme for teaching infants to read which consists of such cards. Quite a number of teachers think that those words which are not pronounced exactly as they are spelled have to be taught as "sight words".

We must therefore review just what we expect of a child when we try to teach him to read, or even to recognize a limited number of words, by a sight method. His task will be a difficult one—I can even say impossible—on four counts.

First, the shapes of words in English, being mere strings of letters along a line, are not distinctive enough. If the teacher, as reading specialists used to advise, draws a line around the outer edge of each word, she will produce exactly the same shape for different words—for example *word* and *sent*, *young* and *going* would produce the same outline. If the child tries looking at the pattern made by the individual letters, he will have to make an enormous number of detailed comparisons in order to distinguish between words like *word* and *wood*, *start* and *stand*, *blend* and *blind*. It will probably take him a long time to realize that the difference of one small letter is all

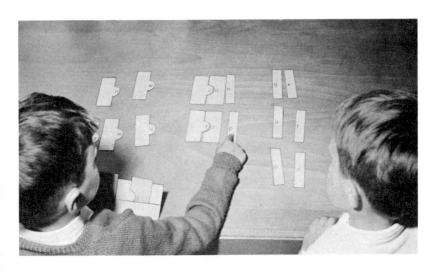

*By playing with the Half-Moon
Cards children learn to fuse
sounds into larger groupings. The
interlocking half-moon shapes
provide a pattern for easy and
instantaneous blending; this does
away with the laborious and
artificial "building up" of words
from separate sounds.*

that important, and he will need well-practised perceptual skills. Obviously the child who has not learned to attend closely to what he sees will never make any progress by this method. The truth is that our writing was never meant to be read as if it were a picture language.

Some Kindergarten and Grade One teachers feel that it is a good thing to give young children a number of words to recognize by sight, so that they may get the idea of what reading is about. I would not object to this provided the words chosen are such as can be used to illustrate the phonic principle, and that from the very beginning the teacher draws the children's attention to the sounds of the beginning letters. The danger arises if she does succeed in training the children to treat the shapes of the word as a clue. She is then leading them up a blind alley of learning. A child who keeps on trying to identify words by their shapes will get into a frightful state of confusion and frustration.

Let us suppose that an observant and attentive child taught by a sight method achieves some success by using the individual letters as distinctive signs. The words given to him will probably not be the very similar pairs, like the examples given above, so that at the beginning he will make encouraging progress. Perhaps he learns to recognize some fifty words. As the number increases, finer and finer discriminations have to be made and there is an increasing risk that somewhat similar words will be confused. Before long the new words the child learns begin to erase the memory of those he learned earlier. Let the reader who still needs convincing try to do the same thing with a number of words written in shorthand. He will find that he needs some kind of system of tags by which to classify the words. In a phonetic script the obvious thing to do is to relate the beginning parts of the words with the beginning sounds. Almost certainly this is what happens when a child makes any considerable progress on a sight method. Either consciously or unconsciously he discovers the phonic code for himself. But how much more sensible to present the child with groups of words beginning with similar sounds, then arrange some activity by which he quickly notices the bonds between sounds and letters!

The final and overriding drawback of a sight method of learning to read is that the child has no means of deciphering new words for himself. He is dependent upon being told what each word is. Every time he forgets it—and permanent learning usually involves forgetting and learning again—someone has to tell him afresh. When there is a system at hand by which he can work out the words himself, this amounts to sheer stupidity.

The phonic method   Let us then agree that we should teach the child by a phonic method. Here, however, there are also pitfalls, because the mental processes required are not quite what they seem to be. We can describe what happens by imagining that we are teaching a robot computer to read. First we programme it to split every word up into a number of what we may call vocal or sound atoms. Let us suppose that we say the word *spit* to our computer. It registers the hiss of

95

the *s* as its first sound atom. As soon as the explosive *p* occurs it recognizes the next one, and so on, recording not only the way the breath is controlled to produce the atoms, but also the length of time taken up by each. Then we show the computer the written word, and programme it so that it links each of the sound atoms with a letter. We ask it to play them back to us. Since it has recorded them exactly as they were pronounced by a human being, the word *spit* emerges. We might then test the programming by asking the computer to produce the sound atoms in a different order. When we show it the words *tips, pits, sips, pips* it is able to read them because the sound atoms are fairly standard from one word to another. So long as we show it only phonetically regular words the computer will be able to read them all with no problems. Sequences of sound atoms will be brought out of its store in the order provided by the letters, and will be re-fused to emerge as natural words.

There is no doubt that this is how a child's brain works in mastering the phonic code. Henceforth I will speak of a "computer-brain" to refer either to our imaginary computer or to the real brain. In the brain the decoding of the letters of a written or printed word occurs just as rapidly as in a computer. (Later we shall see that the brain learns to code the sounds by groups or chunks of sounds, but this is an extension of the same process.)

Suppose that a child is introduced to the phonic principle in quite a different way. He is set to learn what are generally called "the sounds of the letters", pronouncing each separately as *ah, bu, cu, du,* etc. These take many times longer to pronounce than our

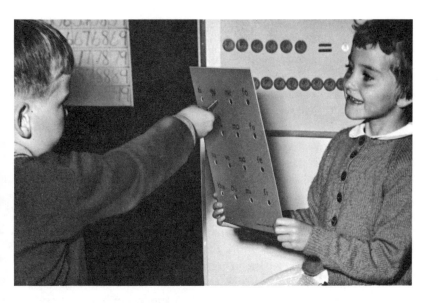

*Children find the Port-Holes a
fascinating game. One asks where
the picture is; then the other
pushes his pencil through the
hole beside the two beginning
letters of the word. This gives
them practice in learning the two
sounds as a unit.*

sound atoms. Nevertheless the computer-brain of the child is programmed to note and store these as sound atoms of the phonic code. When it is given a word—say *cat*—and it plays back the *cu, ah, tu,* the result is a three-syllabled bit of nonsense. It is quite unlike the word *cat* because the mini-syllables which are fused together are not the true sound atoms of which the word is composed.

What happens next depends upon how insistent the search section of the child's brain is in sorting out the muddle. It will inevitably work in part by trial and error, just as when a watch won't go we give it a shake, or if an object won't fit into a box we try it another way round. Perhaps it tries trimming down the *cu-at-tu* to the true sound atoms and fuses them together. Alternatively, it may make an entirely fresh start, and worry out the connection between the sound atoms and the letter itself. Perhaps just one such linkage gives it a clue. When a written word begins with the letter *c*, the spoken word nearly always starts with the same explosive sound as does *cat*. The search section is encouraged and decides to find out whether the same applies to the ways other words begin. The trick is found to apply to letter after letter. The mysterious code has been broken. Progressively the whole code is built up, and when it is played back, true natural-sounding words emerge. For most young computer-brains the search has a happy ending, because in one way or another, they find the key to the reading of words. But they had to discover it for themselves.

The reader may wonder, since we cannot peer into the mind of the child, how I can be so confident about what happens when a child masters the phonic code. It first dawned upon me when I listened to children who had been taught to tackle new words by a sight method. One girl, who was brought to me as a living example of the effectiveness of this method, got stuck for a moment at the word *silver*. Then, with methodical deliberateness, she pronounced each syllable separately: *sil-ver*. It was evident that she was using the phonic code to produce the sounds at nearly their natural spoken rate. Whether she knew what she was doing or not did not matter, because the rapid mental operations that I have described take place automatically and unconsciously. Only the completely formed word comes into consciousness.

Confirmation of this explanation came to me when I visited an old-fashioned rural school in which the teacher was still using the alphabetic method. This consists in getting the child to sound out, not the *ah, bu, cu, du* of our early grades, but the actual names of the letters, *ay, bee, see, dee*. A child spells out *ar, ay, bee, bee, igh, tee*—and immediately says "rabbit". It worked, at least for most children. But how? Quite evidently the names of the letters could not have been fused to make *rabbit*. Therefore some other decoding process must have taken place. It is no more sensible to think that the *ah, bu, cu, du* mini-syllables can be fused into true words; some other decoding process must take place alongside them. This it is that supplies the word. The building up that the child does at the request of the teacher is a kind of incantation which is thought to be necessary to produce the word. But it is no more part of the process itself than is the spell recited by a savage

99

over a cooking pot.

What is the significance of all this for you as a parent in teaching your child to read? It means, first, that you should not teach him the so-called sounds of the letters as a drill. You may, if you like, treat *ah, bu, cu, du* as the names of the letters instead of *ay, bee, see, dee*; and if his teacher does so it would be best to follow suit. But don't give your child the impression that they are the sounds that words are built up with, and above all don't try to make him blend them together to make words. The child who lacks confidence is apt to fasten on to the sounding-out ritual and won't let it go. Reading for him becomes a recitation of these sound syllables; this prevents him from attending to the meaning, and is one of the worst habits to remedy later. And remedy it one must, for the backward reader will never make any progress as long as he sounds out every unfamiliar word.

You should avoid colourful but misleading ways of describing how letters stand for sounds. A friend of mine, the Principal of a Teachers' College, told me that she had not learned to read until she was eleven. She had been told *to listen to the sounds that the letters were saying*. She listened, and hearing nothing, concluded that she must be suffering from some peculiar type of letter-deafness. Then, one day, she walked up the stair of a subway, on the rise of every step of which was written an advertisement for a popular laxative. She found herself saying the words! From that moment she could read anything. Beneath the level of consciousness her brain had collected evidence about the correspondence of the atom

1	met	mix	mop	mud	mad
2	tip	top	⬤	⬤	tap
3	rug	red	rich	rock	rag
4	⬤	hen	⬤	hot	⬤
5	pot	pat	pet	pit	puff

Pattern Bingo is another game
for listening to the first two
letters. Listening to the first
letter only is not enough because
all the words in a line begin with
the same one.

sounds and the letters of words, and at a suitable opportunity, with the words of the advertisement repeated perhaps twenty times, the decoding stage was tried, and it worked.

What you should do is to help your child programme the true code into his computer-brain. You will not be able to do this by pronouncing the sounds and pointing to the letters, because the sounds, as we have seen, are unpronounceable separately. He has to learn to hear them as parts of naturally spoken words.

Teaching the basic sounds
Start first with the beginning sounds, since he will be able to identify these most easily. In the Programmed Reading Kit we begin with the Touch Cards. I will not explain in detail here how they are used because the Manual does so. In the picture on page 23 of this book you can see two children with some of these cards in holders. One child asks, "Where is the cow (or gate, or tiger)?" The other child must say the word *cow* to himself, listen to the first sound, and then pick the card with the *c* on it. He turns it over to see if there is a picture of a cow on the other side. Before long the children will be snapping up card after card as their learning partners name the objects, without pausing to say the word to themselves, and they will be getting them right. The computer-brain has been programmed. It holds in its store an atom sound which, when fused with others in the order of the letters of a word, causes a word to be said, effortlessly and instantaneously, without any laborious "building up".

Several learning stages have to be gone through,

however, before that happy state of affairs comes to pass. Having learned that behind the *m* card will be monkey, he has to realize that the letter *m* is the clue to other words beginning with the "monkey sound". In the First-letter cards, illustrated on the same page, the *m* card will, besides *monkey,* have the words *matches, mat* and *moon.* Then the child needs to generalize this connection to all words that begin with *m*. The First-letter Bingo and some writing games help him to do this. Ideally, at this stage, he will look around his home to find still more *m, s, t,* words and so on. You and he can play the traditional game of "I spy with my little eye something beginning with *m (s, t,* etc.)". The asking player looks in the direction of the object; the other player follows his eyes and guesses which object beginning with the sound is in the asking player's mind.

Coding by larger chunks When your child has become quick at linking words with the correct beginning letters he is ready to go on to the next stage. This is not yet the decoding of complete words. Linguists have shown us that in every language sounds are grouped in standard combinations. For example, the word *standard* is made up of a very common combination *st*, which is itself part of a still quite common larger one *stan. Combination* contains the basic *co,* which here occurs as part of the syllable *com*, but occurs in other words in the syllables *cob, cod, col, con, cos,* etc. These groupings allow the computer-brain to accept two or more sounds as one programming unit. Instead of having to fuse *sta* afresh each time, it

103

learns to respond with the readymade syllable. This makes the decoding process much more rapid. The girl who read *sil-ver* had spontaneously reached this stage.

As with the coding by the individual sounds, we cannot perform this combining stage for the child, but we can help him to achieve it for himself. Just as he had to build his own code by listening to beginning sounds and linking them with letters, so now he has to learn to combine the individual sound atoms into units of two or three sounds. We help him to do this by playing with the Half-Moon Cards, illustrated on page 93. The interlocking moon-shaped edges of the cards act as a demonstration of this process. It is, quite literally, a device for programming his computer-brain to arrange the individual sounds into the standard groupings. Once he has done this he will have overcome the biggest stumbling block for the slow learner, namely the fusing (or blending) of sounds to make words. And it will simply have happened, without being a stumbling block for him at all. Progressively, he learns to programme in still larger chunks of sounds, and finally whole words. When he has built up a stock of a good number of these he will be a fluent reader.

The phonic conventions For a language like ours, in which the spelling is not phonically regular, this ability to accept groups of letters as coding units has a further advantage. The special combinations which stand for sounds different from those of the letters which represent them—*ow, igh, kn, ate, tion,* etc.—can also

The Snakes Games teach those
sounds which are written with
special letter groupings, such as
aw, ea, ow, igh. Each Snake game
deals with only one sound, and
this is contained in the name of
its color. Thus the White Snake
has all eye sounds, the Brown
Snake has all ow sounds, the Blue
Snake oo sounds.

be accepted as coding units in their own right. The child whose brain is active enough to notice these for himself will in the course of time build up his own secondary code of what we call the phonic conventions (it is a convention, for example, that the *tion* in this word and in many other words is pronounced *shun*). That this happens unconsciously becomes clear when we realize that every fluent reader uses this secondary code but few could write it out.

Helping the learning-disabled child to programme his brain

We cannot, however, leave the learning-disabled child to build up this secondary code by himself. In the Programmed Reading Kit it is systematized in the Colour Sound Cards. The name of the colour of the card acts as a reminder for the sound. The Brown card contains words with the sound as in *brown*, the Gold card those as in *gold*, and so on. The same device is used in the Snakes Games (page 105), each colour of snake giving practice in the different ways in which the sound can be written.

Alert, reflective children who use their brain to good effect do their own systematizing in the same way as they build up their own true code of the individual sounds and letters. The unforthcoming child lacks the determination to organize the chaotic mass of sounds into a useable code, so we have to organize it for him. This means pairing up the elements of the code, presenting him with a few at a time and seeing that he learns them thoroughly before going on to the next stage. Seldom will he be unable to make the connections themselves. It is rather that he becomes bewildered if he has to seek them out for himself. The inconsequent child will be at a disadvantage because he does not give himself time to do the searching, nor, when he has some of the connections in his store, to bring them into use.

By providing these children with a "packaged deal" we not only expedite their reading, we bring reading within the reach of some of those who would probably never otherwise learn to read at all. This applies particularly to those children who, because of their extreme unforthcomingness, inconsequence or other behavioural handicap, have been placed in schools for the trainable retarded.

When is a child ready to learn to read? When a child is ready to learn to read depends chiefly upon whether he knows how to learn. But it also depends upon the way he is taught. Dogmas to the effect that a child cannot master the phonic basis of reading until he reaches a mental age of six years are valid only so long as an unrealistic method of teaching phonics is used. The average child can master the phonic code as soon as he has settled down in Kindergarten, provided the pairing of the sounds with their letters is presented to him in an organized programmed sequence. More than once I have gone into a Kindergarten and asked the teacher to let me have her ten slowest children. With the Giant Touch Cards (larger replicas of the ordinary Touch Cards) I teach them first to listen to the beginning sounds, then to notice the shapes of the letters, and finally to link these with the sounds. There may of course be a child or two who suffers some incapacitating disability, but the usual outcome is that every one of them can learn the sound values of four letters in one game session. We found that the children whom we selected from the Retarded Nursery could do so too, prior to their entry into Kindergarten. If I were asked to judge at what age it is best to begin to teach the average child to read by realistic phonic methods, I would say as soon as he has thoroughly mastered speech and is looking around for a new major jump forward, that is to say, at the age of four.

If he can he can With the child about whom we have doubts we first take him through the Learning-to-learn programme. If he shows that he can manage the later stages, the Eight-piece Animal Puzzles and the Matchers Cards, we slip in a reading game as a variant. This will involve the Touch Cards. If he can hear the beginning sounds and pick the right pictures he is on the way to mastering the phonic code. Naturally we proceed very slowly, making sure that each stage is thoroughly practised in a variety of games; in between he plays games of other types, perhaps learning number concepts. If we see that he is still too undeveloped mentally, or too disorganized in his behaviour, to give the necessary attention, we would of course not attempt to take him any further. No harm has been done because to him it was only a game, and he probably enjoyed guessing where the pictures were. He has not been pressured and was unaware of any failure. In fact, I can recall no instance of a child who can manage the Flying Start programme and yet fail on the phonic Touch Cards. Some slow-learning children indeed take to the latter very well, even though the reflectivity demanded of the Matchers Cards is beyond them. So the answer, as always, is to test a child's ability, in phonics or at anything else, by working with him.

If he reaches his limit, the phonic programme can be discontinued for the time being. Even then, his progress up to that point need not be regarded as wasted. Mechanical rote learning, like the recognition of words on cards without any understanding of the phonic principle, is soon erased. Indeed the same words are usually not recognized when seen in a different place or in a different sort of print. But learning based on understanding sticks, because what we call understanding is the brain's method of classification and storage. In one of my Saturday morning reading classes I had a nine-year-old mongoloid girl, who made very slow but steady progress, and reached the stage where she could fuse the individual sounds into the standard groupings such as I have described above. Then she had to spend seven months in hospital, without any reading tuition. When she returned I expected to have to start again at the beginning with her, but she was actually slightly better than when she went into hospital.

Many retarded young people go on developing well into their twenties, as their temperamental handicaps diminish. Not infrequently I have come across retarded young men and women who have taught themselves to read in adulthood. No doubt they could have been taught to read in their teens by the right methods; but merely to have acquired an elementary phonic understanding at that period of their lives would have stood them in good stead later.

A progress plan There is no excuse for letting
for every slow children and young people, clas-
learner sified as retarded, vegetate in an
environment designed on the as-
sumption that they are, and ever will be, incapable of
intelligent learning. I am keenly aware that in writing
like this to you, especially if you are one of those
parents who feel that your child is being retained in
such an unstimulating environment, I shall be accused
of arousing false hopes and putting you in a state of
militant yet impotent frustration. It need not turn
out like that. What your child's school owes you is a
carefully considered progress plan for him. The plan
should lay down a minimum and a best possible goal,
and name the programme that will be used. If you are
allowed to visit his class at regular intervals (and
perhaps work with him in school) you will be able to
convince yourself that the best is being done for him.

Along with our reading programme we have a progress Card upon which the child crayons in each
section that he masters. That for the Flying Start
Learning-to-learn Kit has spaces for the recording of
the child's progress lesson by lesson. The teacher or
other adult in charge not only notes his achievement
in the sense that he has been able to do this or that
puzzle or match the pictures correctly, but also notes
the type of approach he uses—whether he took his
own decisions or wanted encouragement, or whether
he took time to think out the answer or guessed.

Assessing the child's learning style We have a guide, "The Child's Learning Behaviour", which describes all the varieties of faulty approach that we have been able to observe. The degree of handicap that they cause is rated on a scale of from one to three. The teacher consults this, and enters a number against the code-word for the faulty style. This shows the Principal, the psychologist and the teacher herself to what extent over the months the child is overcoming his bad learning habits. Thus part of the progress plan might be to help a child who gets a *3* for "cannot be persuaded to take time to look or think out an answer" to advance to an *1*—"sometimes doesn't 'use his eyes' and guesses when he meets a difficulty". Except for the objective record of his learning style over a period of time the fact that he had advanced from being an always-guesser to a sometimes-guesser would have been missed. Naturally we would hope that in the course of time he would tackle every task methodically and reduce his guessing handicap to zero. But the cure of bad learning habits which originate from weaknesses of temperament may take years.

The use of the Guide provides a basis for productive cooperation between psychologist, teacher and parent in a way that formal tests cannot. It will enable you as the parent to satisfy yourself, with complete realism, that your child is being stimulated to do the best that he is capable of at the time. There can be no false hopes because you will be able to see for yourself, and your frustration will be dissipated in the face of a practical plan of action.

111

The lazy reader   In one of the remedial reading programmes at our Centre we accepted a group of teenage youths and girls who had a certain reading ability in the sense that they could make their way haltingly and inaccurately through a text, but they had no effective reading ability. As usual, we put them through the regular phonic games programme in order to detect the gaps and weaknesses that always exist in such students. They went through it quickly, and arrived at the point where we could say that they had mastered the mechanics of reading. But they didn't bother to read. For years they had used all sorts of subterfuges to avoid reading. One boy made himself so helpful that it took a little time for us to realize that the helpfulness was his strategy of avoidance. These students would no doubt have been given library reading time at school, but it takes a very persistent teacher with unusually strong nerves continually to check that every one of her students uses his time in profitable reading. The result is that they never achieve the easy fluency which would enable them to forget the actual reading process and free their minds to attend to the content. Naturally also, they will never read for pleasure.

What happens to these lazy readers? Most drop out of school at the first opportunity and we do not normally find out whether they ever achieve effective reading. I suspect they do not. During the war an alarmingly large number of recruits were found to be non-readers, and I found the same applied to youths committed to training schools. In both cases, when they entered reading programmes, their instructors

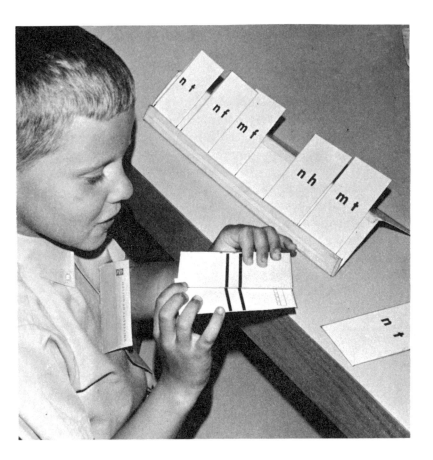

*Some of the series of Matchers
involve discriminating between
letters of the alphabet, like* b *and*
d, *and* m *and* n. *After he has
made his choice the child turns
the cards over and the bars on
the backs tell him if he is correct
or not.*

boasted that they had taught them to read in a few weeks. Teaching a genuine adult illiterate to read is a long and painstaking job. What these instructors had done was to revive their forgotten reading ability. There is thus reason to believe that most students who finish their schooling without fluent reading allow what reading skill they have to fall into disuse. For practical purposes they become illiterates.

Having diagnosed the problem with our group of lazy readers, we wrote the following prescription: regular inescapable reading time, (which became abbreviated to r.i.r.t.). Each individual was allowed to choose his own book and, having read it, had to write down his opinion of the story or other content on a special reading card provided. This showed at a glance which books he had read and the dates he began and finished. We did not use a formal reward system because we found that the students appreciated our interest if we just walked round and discussed each book with them in an informal, friendly way, as if we were discussing the progress of a bench job. Once they became absorbed in a book, they were surprised and encouraged at how quickly fluency came. They had never thought of reading as a source of enjoyment before.

Some 25 years ago, when I renounced the teaching of modern languages in highly academic secondary schools to work with the non-academic type of student, I was put in charge of a class of 14-year-old boys who, against their hopes and expectations, found themselves still having to attend school. The compulsory leaving age had been raised that year to 15, and they had been "caught". I decided that the only thing to do was to build a programme around each of them according to their future jobs. Each compiled a project book. A boy who was to enter his father's fish shop made drawings and wrote descriptions of every conceivable kind of edible fish. It involved a great deal of purposeful reading. In a club within a training school for delinquent youths I built up a technical library and adopted the same plan. Always, a large part of the students' motivation was the regular consultation with an adult who showed an interest in their efforts.

Similarly, if your son or daughter is a lazy reader, what will really count is the interest you show. This may need endless patience, without nagging or bullying. Go to some trouble to find out the right level of reading material both in difficulty and what interests him. Show him how he can follow sports better or learn more about his hobby by being able to read. In consultation with him, you should buy the right kind of book or magazine. Don't object if he prefers comics which appeal to his more primitive instincts. What matters is the habit of reading—even sitting down quietly reading nothing but the captions of comic strips. Try to insist that there should be a regular reading hour each evening. Be around to help him whenever he needs it, but don't stand over him. See that your company is agreeable to him. Don't make him read aloud to you, but if he wants to, listen patiently. In short, let him have constant evidence of your concern and willingness to put yourself out on his behalf. Hypocritical interest will soon be detected. Finally, score your performance secretly from time to time on the Parent-Teacher Self-rating Scale.

Conflict with school learning Parents who wish to help their children at home are often reluctant to do so because they fear they might teach them something which conflicts with what they learn at school. This can happen with procedures such as subtraction in arithmetic, which are usually taught as rules of thumb ("Borrow one and pay it back."). It applies indeed to anything taught mechanically, that is to say, without understanding. If, however, as a result of your teaching, your child understands why something is done in a certain way, you can do no harm. Learning to count offers a good example. The child has to grasp the idea that each numeral in the series represents one more than the preceding one. If he is taught to count mechanically without understanding this, he will not see why he has to start at one or why he should not, for variety's sake, skip a number or change their order now and then. Worst of all, if he thinks counting consists merely in reciting a string of numbers as he would recite a nursery rhyme, it may be difficult for the teacher to develop his counting skill by studying quantities, because he thinks he knows it all already.

The same principle applies in your teaching him to read. If you lead him to understand that the letters represent the sounds that he hears in words, you cannot possibly conflict with what he learns in school because this is the central concept of the phonic code which every would-be reader has to achieve at some level of consciousness. There is no other useful concept that could conflict with it. Even if his teacher is using a sight method no harm will be done because his phonic understanding, even if applied only to the initial letters, will serve him as a tag by which to remember the words. He will thus do better with his teacher. If, however, you also rely on a sight method and give him different words from those he gets from his teacher, he will arrive somewhat sooner at the state of perceptual indigestion that sight methods bring about. The sensible thing to do, of course, is to discuss with his teacher what you propose to do, and coordinate your efforts.

10

The older poor reader

A surprisingly large number of
mothers wrote to me as a result
of Sheena Paterson's article in *Weekend Magazine*
and my radio broadcasts asking what to do about
their adolescent sons who cannot effectively read. As
I said in the last chapter, we have no statistics about
how many young men and women, in the years after
they leave school, cease to use what reading they
have and become virtual illiterates. These letters
confirmed my feeling that the number is larger
than is generally believed. One reason for public
unawareness of the problem is that these young people usually take great care to hide their illiteracy. They
will avoid the type of job in which even occasional
reading is required. I have heard of their suddenly
quitting a job when some change of practice involved
the reading of instructions. Naturally only a narrow
range of jobs is open to them, and they are in the
occupational group where there is most unemploy-
ment. In some instances they are afraid to go out

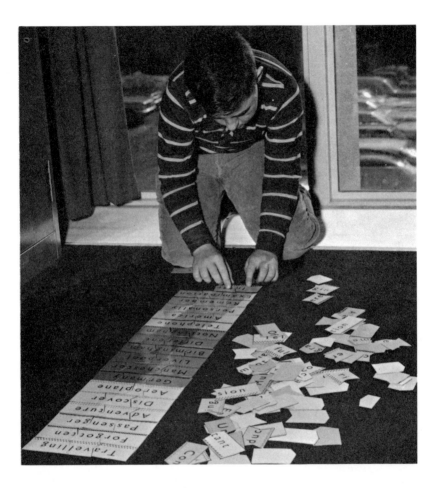

This student is making long words by doing the Long-Word Jigsaws. The cuts between the pieces show him how to break a long word into parts that he can read.

with a girl (or a boy) lest they have to admit they cannot read. In short, their illiteracy, and the shame of it, induces them to lead restricted, unnatural, unproductive lives.

It is unlikely that many of these teenagers or young adults will agree to accept tuition from their parents. Although they may not feel themselves completely grown-up, they want to run their own lives and be as independent as they can. Sitting down to learn to read with a parent would be too like being a child again. Nor is it fair to ask them to go back to school and sit with young children.

The difficulty with many adolescent non-readers is that they have passed the stage when they want to learn to read. They have come to terms with their illiteracy by a process of avoidance. They shut out its disadvantages from their minds, and may even persuade themselves that they are going to manage all right. Many avoid the issue to the extent of not thinking about it at all. With some of them it may take a year or two out in the world to awaken a desire to learn to read.

An educational club   Obviously some special solution is needed which overcomes their sensitivities. It must not directly involve the parents, and it must be quite unlike school. One way of getting around the feelings of shame and isolation is to bring a group of older poor readers and illiterates together in some kind of remedial group.

Many years ago, with the help of a number of special-education teachers and social workers, I ran a small educational club for young people and adults. Along with the usual recreational activities such as table tennis and handicrafts, there was what we tactfully called a Reading Improvement Group. (We borrowed the name from an army class for illiterates.) This was always one of the most popular club activities. We recruited our club members for the most part from youths and girls who had just left or were about to leave school. Their class teachers nominated them from their knowledge of their reading disability, and usually brought them along to the club. Ideally, the boy or girl was invited to join the club during his last months at school and continue after he left. Once the club was established, the social workers who helped out could bring along young adults whom they met or heard of in the course of their regular professional work.

This may prompt you as a parent of an older poor reader to think about getting such a club started in your neighbourhood. The best thing would be to obtain the help of some organization which is actively interested in community problems and could be a source of volunteer club helpers. I have in mind the Association for Children with Learning Disabilities, the National Association for Mental Health or a University Women's Club. You should be able to get the use of premises from your local school board or church, and some financial support from service organizations. The latter may also be able to provide transportation volunteers to collect club members who live in outlying parts, who suffer from a physical disability or who are too shy or otherwise temperamentally handicapped to come on their own. In all cases the organizer of the club should work very closely with the school board and the secondary schools.

Teaching reading to adolescents and adults In our club we learned a great deal about how to teach reading to adolescents and adults. With the emotional resistance that nearly all of them had built up over the years, many found struggling through even the simplest Readers distressing. The task became even more humiliating if the Readers contained pictures of young children and the print was very large. (Children learn how to assess the grade for which a Reader is intended by the size of the type.) On the other hand, they were very willing to play the games of the Programmed Reading Kit. After all, adults play card games. And those in the Kit are programmed so that the students are not faced with a dozen difficulties at once, as when they are reading a text. The Kit was actually built up in the course of my tutoring a group of teenage illiterate youths. When I started with them they flatly refused to work with books. Not only were they not ashamed to play the games, they were even proud when other students gathered round as spectators.

With students of this age, even if they have some reading ability, reading to the tutor from a book is unwise until they are able to manage it with ease. The vital transition to book-reading is made in the Programmed Reading Kit by first presenting the student with a story—in this case a fable—in seven sections on cards. On the back of each card are the common irregular words found in the text on the other side. Once the student can read the cards and the irregular words he is given an expanded version of the same fable in a book. He finds that he knows nearly all the words and can rip through it. By a reconditioning process his old fear of books is overlaid by a new and pleasurable experience. Reading can be easy!

"Pattern of English" We have just now completed an experimental edition of a learning-to-write kit that we call "Pattern of English". It consists of sections of sentences on hinges which can be turned over and matched. The student's task is to construct and write down as many sentences as he can from the parts in any one set. In playing a game with another student, neither can re-use a sentence part used already. The programme starts with very simple sentences, the verbs of which are *is, are, has, have*. Step by step, adjectives and adverbs are added, and past tenses and the question and command forms of the verbs are introduced. Finally, as the students run out of sentence parts, they are allowed to think of their own. In this way they learn original writing with the sentence pattern in their minds.

11

Epilogue

As soon as one proposes anything one finds that somewhere someone is doing it, or doing something better, already. These people, who have worked out good solutions unaided, do not take the time off to write about them. Many do not realize that they are social or educational innovators, and so they hide their light under a bushel. I should be delighted to have reports of their enterprise in order to be able to pass on, with due credit, the solutions they have worked out. I should also like to hear, in due course, how any suggestions I have made in this book have worked out.

To save misunderstandings and possible disappointments I feel I ought to say something about the nature of our Centre and my own work. The Centre for Educational Disabilities at the University of Guelph is primarily a research organization. We accept groups of children from nearby school boards in connection with the new remedial programmes that we develop. It is in this context only that we give remedial treatment. We have not the staff to advise in individual cases, and none of us work privately for fees. I do not myself do any private consultative work.

If you as a parent feel that your child is not getting adequate help, the first thing to do is to discuss your concern with the Principal of his school. He will no doubt draw upon the services of a special education consultant or school psychologist if such are available. I am aware as I write this that many boards do not have adequate facilities in special education. It is not entirely their fault because of the shortage of suitably qualified personnel. This results from the failure on the part of governments to recognize the extent and gravity of the problem, and their consequent failure to provide adequate training facilities. Our universities are also to blame for neglecting to set up enough programmes in special education. It is claimed in their defence that they are there to educate, not to provide professional training. My answer is that it is possible to do both. The field of learning disabilities is notably one in which the college student can educate himself in how the human mind and behavioural system work. One cannot learn the how and why of people's behaviour solely from experimentation in a laboratory. The reasons for our actions have to do with real life, and indeed behaviour has evolved as a characteristic of animals (including man) because of the real-life advantages it has brought. Remove the person from real situations where he has desires, goals, and fears, and the very term behaviour loses its meaning. The universities cannot study life by removing themselves from life.

While this controversy rages, you have a growing

child. Time is not on your side if he has a learning disability. No one can gainsay your right to do your best for him. If there is no professional help available you may decide to teach him yourself, or to organize community support for voluntary facilities. It is because I know that few parents have the necessary skills, and because I am aware of the danger of their making the attempt without guidance, that I have written this book.

If you do decide to act as teacher to your own child it is nonetheless advisable to let his teacher know what you are doing. I do not think you need fear discouragement. Up until a few years ago it was the policy of boards to keep parents, as far as possible, off school premises. This had many unfortunate results. Generally, the Principal and the class teacher only saw parents when they felt they had a grievance. Many parents, especially those who had left school early and did not cherish sweet memories of it, were afraid to visit the school at all, and only did so when they were so angry that they came resolved to have a row. Both sides only saw the worst of each other. Being strangers, they easily slipped into a state of mutual and unfounded suspicion. Fortunately all that has changed. Many schools now even welcome the parents into the classroom, where they can observe what is going on, see how their children set about learning, and perhaps work directly with their children under the teacher's guidance. There is immense scope for further developments in cooperation between parents and teachers. One form this could take would be for the parent to give individual tuition to the child with the teacher's knowledge and

The purpose of the Matcher's Game is to teach the child to think out a problem rather than guess at it. As he is given each card he has to find the match from among the row of six. He has to notice more than one difference—not only whether the pirate is wearing a hat, but whether he has a wooden stump for a leg, and if so whether it is the right or the left leg.

guidance. The day may not be far off when schools actually undertake the responsibility of training parents to help their children at home.

Parents' organizations have contributed much to getting better facilities for the education of learning-disabled and retarded children. Also, they have been a tremendous source of comfort to their members by breaking the sense of isolation which the parents of such children are apt to feel. It is always a great help to get to know people who have similar problems to one's own. Further, I think that the value of parents' organizations is tremendously increased when they provide positive activities in cooperation with the schools.

One such positive activity is the formation of a parents' tutorial group. This can either offer its services to schools, or the members can set up their own tutorial circle to teach their own and each others' children. One practical advantage of the existence of such a group is that much expense can be saved by the cooperative purchase of materials. This applies particularly to the kits of learning games. Each child may need to use an item only for a week or two, and the cards will still be as good as new. An enterprising parents' circle could buy a kit cooperatively and lend the items out at a small weekly charge that would pay for the whole in a few months, and perhaps provide a surplus for additional games. Moreover, many of the card materials for these games can be handmade at practically no expense at all. Even if materials are copyrighted to prevent their being pirated by rogue publishers, you are legally entitled to make a copy for your own private use.

Appendix: Learning games

READING

Programmed Reading Kit

This is a graded series of learning games and practice exercises. None of the material is too young in content, so that it can be used with teenagers or even adults. It is packaged in two boxes (Part I and Part II) containing perforated cardboard sheets, which are broken up into the cards used in the games.

Part I starts at the very beginning of phonic understanding, teaching the child to listen to the beginning sounds of words and to link them with letters.

You can buy the first two items of the Kit (the Touch Cards and the First-Letter Cards) separately, and it is best to do this if you are not certain whether your child is ready to make a start with reading. If he is not, you will then be saved needless expense.

Even if your child has a certain reading ability he should begin at Part I. His difficulties almost certainly go back to the very foundations of phonic knowledge, and these must be cleared up before he can make real progress. This applies to young people of any age.

The Manual describes the whole sequence of the program extending over Parts I and II of the Kit. If you follow the directions carefully item by item and you train yourself to be a good tutor by using the Parent-as-Teacher Self-Rating Scale, you should be able to manage without further guidance. On the other hand, there are advantages in studying and practising the games in a group. Even if there is no experienced demonstrator at hand, a group of mothers or volunteers can read the directions for playing each game from the Manual and play among themselves until they become familiar with it.

The games can be played satisfactorily with one child and the adult acting as partner, but ideally they should be played by two or more children by themselves, with the adult at hand to show them how to begin, and to give guidance where necessary.

The chief items of Part I of the Kit, apart from the two mentioned above, are:

exercises and Bingo games to practise the sounds of the letters;

the Half-Moon Cards to teach the child to cope with the first two letters of a word as a unit;

the Port Holes and Pattern Bingo games to practise the handling of two-letter units;

the Which-of-Two game to draw attention to the end-letters of simple words;

the Mail Box game for discriminating between *b, d, p, q;*

two Brick Wall games for the making of simple complete words.

The chief items of Part II of the Programmed Reading Kit are:

the First Sentence Family, which leads the student to the reading of sentences composed of very simple, regular words;

the Fables cards, which introduce the commonest irregular words;

the Colour-Sounds cards, the Snakes games and the Second Sentence Family, which teach and practise all those letter-groupings that are pronounced differently from their separate letters (*ow, ea, ew, oo,* etc.);

the Third Sentence Family, which directs special attention to the long vowels before an unpronounced *e* (don't worry if this seems rather technical: the games teach directly without involving the use of specialized terms);

the Long-Word Jigsaws, which show the learner how to break up long words into smaller groupings.

The *Programmed Reading Kit* is available:
in Canada, from
> Gage Educational Publishing Ltd.
> P.O. Box 5000
> 164 Commander Boulevard
> Agincourt, Ontario

in the United States, from
> Scott Foresman, Ltd.
> Glenview, Illinois, 60025
> (or State depository)

in Great Britain, from
> Holmes, McDougall Ltd.
> 30 Royal Terrace
> Edinburgh EH7 5AL

in Australia, from
> the Australian Council for Educational Research
> P.O. Box 210
> Hawthorn, Victoria

WRITING AND SPELLING

Pattern of English

This Kit consists of a graded series of parts of sentences held together by plastic spines. The student chooses the parts which, when joined, make sense. It can be used by a single student or in a game involving two. In either case the object is to see how many whole sentences can be made. When a student runs out of sentence parts he is encouraged to make up his own. In this way, once he has the pattern of each type of sentence, he learns to apply it in writing to what he wants to say.

Having made a sentence, the student copies it in a book or on a sheet of paper. He scores the point for the sentence only if all the words are spelled correctly. With care, this should give him no difficulty because the words are in the sentence parts. He learns to spell by paying attention to words and writing them, not by learning "spelling" by rote.

The sequence starts with very short, simple sentences using only the verbs *is* and *are*. The next sets are about people doing things. These are subsequently expanded by adding adverbs saying "when". The next group uses two-word verbs such as *is wearing,* and their negative forms. Then there are the sentence forms used in telling people to do things and in asking questions. Finally, double verbs are introduced (*must eat, has eaten, is eaten,* etc.).

There is no attempt to teach any formal grammar. Neither the tutor nor the student needs to know what

133

is meant by nouns, verbs, subjects, objects, etc. The grammar is learned unconsciously, in the same way as the child learns to speak, that is to say, by picking up the word pattern.

This Kit helps the student to overcome his fear of writing. In the beginning he does not have to write an original composition. He comes to do this gradually, as he finds he needs new sentence parts. The Pattern of English Kit is also useful in giving the non-English speaking immigrant models of English sentence structure upon which to base his own speaking and writing.

Pattern of English is available from the Centre for Educational Disabilities, University of Guelph, Ontario.

TRAINING IN GOOD LEARNING HABITS

The Flying Start Learning-to-learn Kit

This Kit has been designed for four-to-six-year-old children, and those of any age who have not learned how to attend, lack the confidence to tackle learning tasks, or are so impulsive that they don't give themselves time to think.

It is packaged in a box of perforated cardboard sheets, which are broken up into the cards needed for playing the games. These are then stored in the kit container provided.

The child works individually with the puzzles, and plays the other games with another child or with an adult.

The programme begins with the simplest possible activities, such as joining together the four quarters —or even the halves—of a boldly drawn picture.

Then follows the Mail Box game, which consists in posting the letters of the alphabet in the correct slots as shown by the letters on the outside. Another child, sitting on the receiving side, checks by matching the half picture on the card posted with the half on the floor of the box.

Using the Merry-Go-Rounds children learn to take turns in playing a game. The making of the Merry-Go-Round circle seems to win the attention of hyperactive children when nothing else interests them.

The Animal Puzzles are so arranged that the child

follows the order of the numbers on their backs in fitting the pieces. This trains him to work in an orderly manner without resorting to trial-and-error.

The Matchers teach the child to bear several considerations in mind before making a decision. He learns that it pays to think out the answer in advance rather than act impulsively.

The Flying Start Learning-to-learn Kit is available:
in Canada, from
> Gage Educational Publishing Ltd.
> P.O. Box 5000
> 164 Commander Blvd.
> Agincourt, Ontario

in the U.S.A., from
> Wardell Associates
> 49 Pinckney Street
> Boston, Mass. 02114

in Great Britain, from
> Holmes, McDougall Ltd.
> 30 Royal Terrace
> Edinburgh, EH7 5 AL

in Australia, from
> The Australian Council for Educational Research
> P.O. Box 210
> Hawthorn, Victoria

NUMBER

The Flying Start Learning-about-Number Kit

This Kit is designed for four-to-six-year-old children, and those of any age who have difficulty in grasping the ideas of counting, quantity and addition.

It begins by teaching the recognition of the numbers and their names. Then the child learns the basic idea of counting—that each number is one more than the last.

The idea of an exact quantity is learned by games in which something goes wrong (a group of children are one ice cream short, etc.) unless the child makes sure he has the right quantity. Other games teach accurate, meaningful counting. Finally, the Number Mail Boxes teach the principle of addition and show the child that he can save himself time in the game by learning the addition facts (6 + 3=9).

The Flying Start Learning-about-Number Kit is available from the Centre for Educational Disabilities, University of Guelph, Guelph, Ontario.

LEARNING LEFT AND RIGHT

Left-Right Pairs

This is a set of cards with 24 pairs of animals, one of the pair facing to the left and the other to the right. The backs of the cards give a clue in the form of a picture of a child raising the left or right hand.

They lend themselves to a variety of games. Very young or retarded children learn to identify the "Noah's Ark" pairs. Older children play a "Concentration" type of game.

Families

This set of cards can be used in a variety of games for children and young people of all ages; some of the games are very simple—of the Fish type; others are more sophisticated.

Two of the series of cards, or Families, to be collected require the making of a distinction between *b* and *d*.

Both the *Left-Right Pairs* and the *Families* Cards can be used as social games as a change from the reading games for young people of any age.

They are available from the Centre for Educational Disabilities, University of Guelph.